ΙRY SERVI

ɘv   +

A TREASURY OF
ANGLO-SAXON ENGLAND

A TREASURY OF
ANGLO-SAXON ENGLAND

FAITH AND WISDOM
IN THE LIVES OF MEN AND WOMEN,
SAINTS AND KINGS

PAUL CAVILL

HarperCollins*Publishers*

HarperCollins*Publishers*
77–85 Fulham Palace Road, London W6 8JB
www.**fire**and**water**.com

First published in Great Britain in 2001
by HarperCollins*Publishers*

1 3 5 7 9 10 8 6 4 2

A catalogue record for this book is available
from the British Library

ISBN 0 00 710403 0

Printed and bound in Great Britain by
Creative Print and Design (Wales), Ebbw Vale

To Rick and Snugs
with love

CONTENTS

INTRODUCTION

Anyone looking at a piece of Anglo-Saxon art will be struck by the patterns. Whether the art is in carved stone, or a page of manuscript illumination, or a personal ornament like a brooch, patterns are there. Some of them are almost overwhelming in their detail and intricacy, like the carpet pages of the Lindisfarne Gospels. Lithe and strange beasts threaten to leap off the page. Some are more sober and stark, like the interlace patterns of decoration on Anglo-Saxon stone crosses, often to be found in neglected corners of old churchyards. But like the visual patterning of Anglo-Saxon art, Old English literature also has patterns. The patterns are there, in rich variety, when you read closely. And they all have meaning.

Patterns connect people with the past, with tradition, inherited values, ways of thinking, styles of worship. Patterns are enjoyed and valued in the present, too. They connect people with one another. Anglo-Saxon art, whether in stone or in verse, is the skill of the individual used for the delight of the community. Patterns are a language which communicates. Beauty and usefulness come together and reflect communal values and needs. At the heart of Anglo-Saxon Christianity is a connection with the past: the Bible, the apostles and patriarchs, the great saints and martyrs, the inherited learning and discipline of the Church. The Anglo-Saxons felt their kinship with the people, and drank in the teaching. But this is all connected to the present, to the everyday life and experience of men and women, abbesses and warriors, smiths and mothers, children and the elderly. In Old English Christian literature poets and writers experience the biblical past in terms of the present.

This book starts with the ordinary things of life in Anglo-Saxon England: the world, families, work, leisure, children and the ways people thought about all these things. With the pleasure and delight, there is a good deal of sadness, because the Anglo-Saxons often lived in harsh conditions. It would be a mistake to miss out the sadness and difficulty, because as the Anglo-Saxons themselves knew, sorrow gives joy its sweetness. Old English literature is robust: poets felt keenly their own miseries and those of others, but looked for consolation, and often held before themselves the prospect of heaven.

Then we move on to the recognized forms of the spiritual life from Anglo-Saxon England: monks and nuns, saints and martyrs. These had their fair share of troubles, too, as the chapters show. But perhaps the main misconception we have about people in the religious life is that on entering it, they give up the endless pressure of decision-making and choosing from the variety of options available in life. Not at all. Within the pattern of established religious life, monks and nuns, priests and bishops, had to make moment by moment decisions about how they would inwardly respond to God and their fellows. The conventional praise of the saint or abbess's goodness in the literature represents decisive commitment in everyday living, the kind of living that is anything but conventional in its daily expression.

'The past,' it is said, 'is another country.' Certainly they do things differently there. Throughout this book I have written of Old English and the Anglo-Saxons as if they were a kind of seamless unity. If we count the Old English period from the middle of the fifth century through to the middle of the 11th, that makes six centuries, the same as the length of time separating us from Geoffrey Chaucer. And though the pace of change was slower, change certainly happened. Monasticism, for example, was very different in seventh-century Northumbria from what it was in 10th-century Wessex. But it is true to say that the Anglo-Saxons shared more in their patterns of thinking and experience with each other, from whatever part of the period, than they do with us. So I have tried not only to explain the way the Anglo-Saxons thought, but also to see some connections between them in the first millennium and ourselves in the third.

This book is a 'treasury', to be dipped into. I have not tried to cover any of the topics systematically, but rather to bring out a few gems to share. There are some delights here, pieces of verse or prose that shine with good sense, or gleam with sharp insight. There is wit and drama, as well as pathos and imagination. There is, to be sure, serious and thoughtful devotion, but it is allied with a lively sense of the privilege of living in a Christian society. I have not always made the points that could be made from the examples I have chosen, but I hope the vitality of Anglo-Saxon expressions of faith and hope and joy will help to strip off some of the layers of familiarity and staleness that many today feel have encrusted Christianity.

There is a place for systematic treatment of Anglo-Saxon Christianity. But my perception is that the Anglo-Saxons were better at practical and biblical theology than they were at systematic theology. Bede was the greatest thinker of his day, but he had too great a respect for his authorities to be original or overly systematic. I suggest, then, that a better image of the essence of Anglo-Saxon Christianity than the system is the pattern. In a pattern there is order, but a pattern normally includes elements of tradition, skill, meaning, development, beauty.

After each topic, I have given a translation of a prayer or a hymn or a meditation, with a few comments. Most of these are from the liturgies of Anglo-Saxon England, and they perhaps give a different view of the topics. At any rate, I offer them as interesting in themselves, and for the meditative focus they bring. I hope, in fact, they will bring a sense of completeness to what is a sketch of vibrant faith.

This is my second book about Anglo-Saxon Christianity. I gave that title, *Anglo-Saxon Christianity*, to an earlier book, not because I imagined it covered all the ground, but because I wanted to demonstrate that Christianity in Anglo-Saxon England was about more than just the church, or the liturgy, or the conversion. In fact, I wanted to argue that Christianity was a way of seeing things that was evident in literature such as heroic poetry, where some scholars either could not discern it, or did not think it was important. I want to do that in this book as well, but with a slightly different focus.

In *Anglo-Saxon Christianity*, I left a great deal of interesting material out of consideration, or only touched on it very lightly. This book, while it starts with general topics illustrating the way the secular Anglo-Saxons thought about their world in Christian terms, goes on to consider the more obviously religious ways of living and dying. It still leaves a lot out: I have not given much from the Old English biblical poems, and only a very little of the great wealth of sermons.

This is partly because these are the 'obvious' things to look at when thinking of Anglo-Saxon Christianity, and the neglected corners of the literature are often more interesting, to me at least. So I am still being very selective, but I still think the material I am dealing with shows the depth and vitality of the faith of the Anglo-Saxons.

1

THE WORLD

For most ordinary people in Anglo-Saxon England, life was hard and often dreary, if not miserable. Things we take for granted which make life pleasant were unknown: warmth in winter, fresh foods all year round, cures for many simple diseases, protection from the elements, clean clothes and sweet-smelling rooms. The Anglo-Saxons were constantly beset by nature in its less agreeable forms. Cold, wet and windy weather is part of the exile's lot, as we shall see in chapter 3, but even for ordinary people it oppresses the mind. Danger from animal savagery is frequently mentioned in the literature, wolves and bears still populated the land. And the hunger and disease that follow each other after bad harvests, are companions that no one wants. The natural world for many Anglo-Saxons was not the world of leisure and enjoyment, of country walks and panoramic views, but rather a place at least potentially dangerous.

THE GLORY OF CREATION

For all this, one of the most common themes in Old English poetry is the glory of God's creation, the wonder and delight

of sun and moon and the seasons, the bounty and variety of
the natural world. The eyes of many were drawn away from
the squalor immediately surrounding them to the sublime and
stately heavenly bodies. They celebrated in song the wonders
they saw. And, as we shall see, their minds were intrigued and
stimulated by the infinite questions that the world raises.

One of the poems of the Exeter Book, the biggest collection of Old English poetry that we have left to us, poses this
riddle:

> I am bigger than this world,
> smaller than a hand-worm, brighter than the moon,
> quicker than the sun. All the seas
> lie in my embrace, and the green expanse
> of the bosom of this earth. I touch the depths,
> I go down under hell, and climb up over the heavens,
> the home of glory; I stretch far
> over the land of the angels; with myself
> I fill up the earth, the old world
> and the ocean far and wide. Say what I am called.

What is bigger than the world and smaller than the smallest
creature in it? What encompasses everything and fills everything and touches every part of everything? The answer is
creation. The alternative given by scholars is 'Nature', but
while the Anglo-Saxons would not see any difference
between the two, for us the latter is perhaps misleading. It is
worth noticing that the observable world of nature in the
poem is *middangeard*, literally 'the middle enclosure'. It lies
between heaven and hell. The world is created by God, but so
are the mystical landscapes of heaven and hell, the depths
and the land of the angels. The idea of a three-tier universe is
very ancient, but here it is clearly Christian. That view of the
world has to be set in a context.

CREATION AND EVIL

The Anglo-Saxons had a particular view of the creation. This was shaped by the biblical story of the Garden of Eden and Adam and Eve in Genesis, but also the logically preceding, but not explicitly biblical, story of the fall of the angels. People knew that Satan and his angels fell from heaven because of their pride, because it was Satan in the form of a snake who tempted Adam and Eve to get his own back on God. Their theological understanding of the natural world hinges on these two stories of the fall of the angels and the creation. The Old English poem on Genesis starts like this:

> It is a great privilege for us that we praise in words
> and love in our hearts the Guardian of the
>   heavens,
> the glorious King of hosts. He is the strength of all
>   powers,
> the head of all the high-created angels,
> the Lord almighty. He has no source and
> no beginning has ever existed for him; and no end
>   will come now
> for the eternal Lord, but he will forever remain
>   powerful
> over the thrones of heaven with his mighty armies.

God deserves our praise, but before the Old English *Genesis* story progresses through the biblical days of creation, it deals with the separate creation, the pride and the fall of the angels under Lucifer, now Satan, and their quest for vengeance against God.

Ælfric, most prolific of the Old English sermon-writers, deals with the 'Beginning of the Creation' in the same way, and makes explicit the reason for it. He wants us to know that God created all things good, but that there is an enemy at work in the created order, who twists and deforms and traps and defiles things, and people with their collusion, for his own purpose.

> God created as a great angel him who is now the devil: but God did not create him as the devil: but when he was wholly fordone and guilty towards God, through his great haughtiness and enmity, then became he changed to the devil, who before was created a great angel. Then would God supply and make good the loss that had been suffered in the heavenly host, and said that he would make man of earth, so that the earthly man should prosper, and merit with meekness those dwellings in the kingdom of heaven which the devil through his pride had forfeited...
>
> Now the heretics say that the devil created some creatures, but they lie; he can create no creatures, for he is not a creator, but is a loathsome fiend, and with leasing [lying] he will deceive and fordo the unwary; but he may not compel any man to any crime, unless the man voluntarily incline to his teaching. Whatsoever among things created seems pernicious and is injurious to men, is all for our sins and evil deserts.
>
> When the devil understood that Adam and Eve were created, that they might with meekness and obedience merit the dwelling in the kingdom of heaven from which he had fallen for his haughtiness, then he felt great anger and envy towards those persons, and meditated how he might fordo them.

Here Ælfric explains why human beings were created: God, like a great Anglo-Saxon lord, feels the loss of the best part of his retinue, so he determines to replace those lost, albeit by lesser creatures. But those creatures will be constantly under the devil's attack and subject to his wiles. All creation points us to God's glory, then, and all evil reminds us of the devil's pride and human sin. This is hardly flattering to human beings, but it goes some way towards explaining to the Anglo-Saxons why there is evil in the world.

The story of *Beowulf* beautifully echoes this pattern of creation. Hrothgar, king of the Danes, has built a splendid hall and lives in stately joy and order in it. His court poet sings of the creation:

> there was the sound of the harp,
> the clear song of the poet. The one who knew how
> to tell the story from far back related the creation
>   of men,
> said that the Almighty made the earth,
> the land shining in beauty, as far as the water
>   surrounds it,
> established the victorious sun and moon
> as lanterns to lighten the land-dwellers,
> and adorned the corners of the earth
> with branches and leaves. He also created life
> for every kind of creature that moves about alive.
> Thus the noble warriors lived happily
> in joys, until a certain one,
> an enemy from hell, began to carry out crimes.
> The fearsome spirit was called Grendel...

Here in miniature is the story of creation played out again. Grendel, the fiendish enemy, is stirred to hateful action from his dark hideout by the song of the poet. The beauty and order of Hrothgar's hall is like the beauty and order of God's new world, and it is devastated by the hellish envy of the enemy. Fortunately for the Danes, a warrior called Beowulf hears of their plight and determines to help them. And so a distant echo of the coming of Christ into the world to save those who suffered the oppression of the devil is heard.

SUN, MOON AND STARS

Much as the Anglo-Saxons loved the earth and its variety and teeming creatures, some of the most delightful verse is about the sun and moon. The heavenly bodies were not just convenient or a matter for occasional remark at this time: they governed life, determining time, work, rest, meals, harvests, health. Several medicinal recipes prescribe exposing the ill person to the sun, and others specify collecting herbs for medicinal use at dawn, so that the power of the waxing sun is imparted to the herbs. Darkness, in both the scholar Bede and in the folklore of the Old English *Maxims*, is the place for robbers, thieves and those who do not want to have their shame exposed.

But it is not only the light for which the Anglo-Saxons loved the sun and moon, it is also for the way they represent the sublime orderliness of the created universe. The sun and moon follow their courses irrespective of the chances and changes of the world, and so image for humanity the sedate splendour of the heavenly realm. They also reveal the glory of God at whose command they shine. A poem called *The Order of the World* reflects on the creation, land and sea, but especially on the sun, in a sustained hymn of praise and wonder:

Listen! In the beginning the high treasure-keeper,
the Father almighty, created heaven and earth,
and the wide expanse of the sea – those visible
 creations
made by the hand of the Lord, which now in their
 three parts
exalt and raise high the glory of the holy One.
For just as he (who well knew how to do it) united
each thing with the others, and all are subject to
fixed principles of organization; so the Guide
 established
various boundaries for them throughout the great
 natural order.
So they shine with his splendour and keep glowing
 with his praise
for ever. They show the glory of the Lord
and the magnificence of his deeds to eternity.
Without wavering, they carry out the eternal word
 of the Lord
in the original place the Lord, the pure Guardian
 of heaven,
established for them, accurately keep
their sublime boundaries. His power draws out
the lights of the heaven, and with them the
 sea-tides.
The Lord of life summons and leads
all created things into the embrace of his unity;
so for him, the gentlest of all judges,
who created this life for us,
praise shines eternally. And this bright light
comes every morning over the misty hills,
to journey, gloriously adorned, over the waves.
And at dawn, beautiful and pleasant,

it comes from the east to generations of
   humankind,
to every living being. The light, brightest of
   flames,
shines forth, and everyone on earth,
to whom the true King of victories has chosen to
   grant
eyesight, can enjoy it.
Then in its glory the magnificent heavenly body
departs in company to the western sky,
until in the evening it crosses over
the expanse of the ocean, and summons forth
   another twilight.
Night follows, and keeps the command
of the holy Lord. The brilliant sun,
the wandering star bright as heaven,
hurries according to God's decree
under the expanse of the earth.
Wherefore, there is no one living so wise
as to be able by his own intellect to understand its
   origin,
or how the bright gold sun passes through the
   depths
in black darkness under the tumult of the waters,
or who among earth-dwellers may enjoy
the light of it after it passes over the sea.

In this poem, the poet delights in the balance of order, variety, and unity in creation. The first part of the extract borrows from Proverbs 8:27–9, where Wisdom speaks of her presence at the moment of creation:

I was there when he set the heavens in place, when
he marked out the horizon on the face of the deep,
when he established the clouds above and fixed
securely the foundations of the deep, when he gave
the sea its boundary so that the waters would not
overstep his command, and when he marked out
the foundations of the earth.

God has established limits for the heavens, the earth, and the
seas by his wisdom. The poet knows his science, too. He
knows, for example, that the tides are determined by the
moon. But the 'laws of nature' are not in the least abstract:
they are the commands of God. And although the principles
of order are fixed by God's immutable command, the poet
makes clear that the rhythms of the natural world respond to
the heavenly Guide, who draws and leads and summons all
things into his loving embrace. The 19th-century hymn-
writer, John Ellerton, expresses similar thoughts:

> The day Thou gavest, Lord, is ended,
> The darkness falls at Thy behest;
> To Thee our morning hymns ascended,
> Thy praise shall hallow now our rest...
>
> The sun that bids us rest is waking
> Our brethren 'neath the wester sky,
> And hour by hour fresh lips are making
> Thy wondrous doings heard on high.

The difference between the older and the newer of these is
that the Old English poet sees creation, and the sun itself, as
praising God by doing his will. It is not only human beings
that praise God. In the words of the *Benedicite*,

> O all ye works of the Lord bless ye the Lord:
> Praise him, and magnify him for ever.
> O ye Heavens, bless ye the Lord...
> O ye Sun and Moon, bless ye the Lord...
> O ye Nights and Days, bless ye the Lord...
> O ye Light and Darkness, bless ye the Lord:
> Praise him, and magnify him for ever.

And so they do in the Old English poem.

LIGHT AND SIGHT

The English climate can sometimes be dreary. This Anglo-Saxon poet heartily agreed with the writer of Ecclesiastes that 'Light is sweet, and it pleases the eyes to see the sun' (11:7). Here, the light of the sun merges with the glory of God's praise, and its beauty and brightness are almost tangible. It is a privilege given to many to see it:

> everyone on earth,
> to whom the true King of victories has chosen
> to grant
> eyesight, can enjoy it.

But he has not granted that to all. The poet of the *Maxims* feels the misery of blindness.

> Happy is the innocent in heart. The blind man is
> deprived of his eyes,
> — clear vision is taken from him – they cannot see
> the stars bright in the sky,
> or the sun and moon. That is painful to him in his
> mind,

a source of anxiety because he alone knows what it
    is like, and he expects no change.
The Lord ordained that suffering for him, and he
    can grant him relief,
healing for the eye, the jewel of the head, if he
    knows him to be pure in heart.

God gives and God takes away. Those beautiful things that
lift the mind, the brightness and splendour of sun, moon and
stars, are denied to some. The richness of the gift of sight is
skilfully captured by the poet's use of a metaphor here, when
he talks of healing for 'the jewel of the head', meaning the
eye. But the first sentence puts this brief passage into a context where that healing is certain: it refers to Matthew 5:8,
'Blessed are the pure in heart; for they will see God'. The consolation of the passage is that the pure in heart will not have
to be satisfied merely with the creation, but will see God, the
Creator himself.

CHRIST THE LIGHT

In Anglo-Saxon hymns as in more recent, Christ is identified
with light. Christ is the light of the world, the one whose
light shines in the darkness. There are variations on this
pleasing theme, from hymns, sermons and the liturgy. Many
of the Latin hymns in the 11th-century Durham Hymnal
have Old English glosses, translations written between the
lines of the Latin, presumably so that monks whose Latin was
a bit rusty could still enjoy the hymns. The full glosses to an
anonymous hymn in the collection run like this:

Night and darkness and clouds
disturbances and tumults of the earth –
light is entering, heaven becoming white,
Christ is coming – all of you, away!

The murk of the earth is torn apart,
struck with a beam of the sun;
and the colour of all things returns
with the appearing of the shining orb.

O Christ! You alone we recognize.
With pure and resolute hearts,
weeping and singing, to you we pray:
heed the thoughts of our minds.

Many things are stained with dyes
that will be cleansed by your light.
O Light of the eastern orb,
lighten with your gracious appearing!

The song is chiefly dependent on Isaiah's prophecy, 'darkness
covers the earth, and thick darkness is over the peoples, but the
Lord rises upon you and his glory appears over you' (60:2).
What is particularly notable here is the fascination with colour,
which we have seen in earlier pieces. The true light brings out
the colours of things in the second stanza; it also reveals the
fake colours that dyes and pigments give to things in the fourth
stanza. In the hymn these images call to mind St Paul's teaching that Christ at his coming 'will bring to light what is hidden
in darkness' (1 Corinthians 4:5), revealing true colours, and
making clear what is fake, but passes for colour in the darkness.
   At Advent, leading up to Christmas, the Anglo-Saxon
church traditionally sang the Latin 'Advent antiphons' or the

'Great O's', so called because they begin with invocations to Christ addressed in his various biblical names and images: O Emmanuel, O Day-star, O Key of David, O King of the nations, and so on. Several of these are translated in J.M. Neale's hymn 'O come, O come, Immanuel'. Neale's version of *O Oriens*, 'O eastern star, the splendour of eternal light, and sun of righteousness: come and shine on those who sit in darkness and the shadow of death', is this:

> O come, Thou Day-spring, come and cheer
> Our spirits by Thine advent here;
> Disperse the gloomy clouds of night,
> And death's dark shadow put to flight.

The antiphon is much expanded by the Old English author of the poem *Christ*. He relates the image of Christ as 'the splendour of eternal light' to the very similar phrase in the Epistle to the Hebrews, which refers to Christ as 'the radiance of God's glory and the exact representation of his being', the one who sustains 'all things by his powerful word' (1:3). The Son of God is the last and by far the greatest of those sent by God as the writer to the Hebrews makes plain, and indeed is the Creator himself. This theme is woven into the fabric of the antiphon:

> O Star of dawn, brightest of the angels
> sent to people on the earth,
> and the true light of the sun,
> brilliant beyond the heavenly bodies, you
>   constantly illuminate
> every time by your own bright presence.
> You, God verily begotten from God,
> are Son of the true Father in the glory of heaven.

Since you have always existed without beginning,
so now, driven by need, your own creation
asks you with confidence to send us
the bright Sun, and come yourself
to enlighten those who have long since
sat here in perpetual night, covered with cloud
and deep darkness, shrouded by sin,
having to suffer the dark shadow of death.
Now in hope we believe in the salvation
brought to hosts by the Word of God,
who was in the beginning with God,
and is co-eternal with God. And now he has
    become
pure and sinless flesh, born of the virgin
to comfort the sorrowing. God was seen amongst us
without sin. The mighty Son of God
and the Son of Man dwelt together in peace
among the people. For this we can constantly say
richly deserved thanks to the victorious Lord,
in that it was his will to send himself amongst us.

The simple, stark image of light coming into a dark world in
the life of Jesus is lovingly expanded here. The Hebrews
parallel allows, indeed invites, the poet to dwell on the nature
of Christ. The poet is also drawn by the light image in the
Nicene Creed:

[I believe] in one Lord Jesus Christ, the only-begotten
Son of God, Begotten of his Father before all worlds,
God of God, Light of Light, Very God of very God,
Begotten, not made, Being of one substance with the
Father, by whom all things were made: Who for us
men and for our salvation came down from heaven,

And was incarnate by the Holy Ghost of the Virgin
Mary, And was made man...

So the poet uses the Bible and the Creeds in all their richness
to honour Jesus in his real humanity and complete divinity.
But there is also a reference to the customary enmity between
rival sons in Anglo-Saxon England, and this is turned on its
head by the peaceful 'dwelling together' of the divine and
human natures of Jesus. The light of heaven has come and
brought light to the earth. And light is indeed sweet.

ANIMALS

The Anglo-Saxons were not sentimental about animals.
Wolves, eagles and ravens picked the corpses clean after bat-
tles. Bears, known for their savage paws, lived in the woods.
Boars could kill with their tusks as readily as men with spears.
Dogs were working animals or scavengers. The Old English
proverb has it that 'it will be a good year when the dog gives
to the raven', that is, when one scavenger gives food to
another – and the thrust of the proverb is that 'pigs might fly'!
Another of the proverbs in the Durham collection is even
more pragmatic, 'the one who wants to run down the hart
cannot care about the horse'.

Nevertheless animals were important to the Anglo-Saxons,
not only in their husbandry and farming, but also in their
imaginations. Many of the Old English riddles are about animals, and in a later chapter we shall see the curiosity of the
poet of the *Maxims* about the ways and habits of animals.
Here is another riddle:

My hall is not quiet, and I myself am not loud
moving about my noble hall. The Lord created us
a journey, a fate together. I am quicker than
   my hall,
at times indeed stronger, but the hall lasts longer.
Sometimes I rest, my hall runs on and on.
I live in it as long as I live;
   if we should separate from each other, I am dead!

The poet starts with a picture of noble life, a busy hall with
the owner quietly going about his business. But then we hear
that the hall is a moving, changeable thing which runs and
lasts, and is quick and strong, though not as quick and strong
as the creature which has to live in it. The fish is to the river
as the owner is to the hall, with a few differences. The poet
takes pleasure in the idea of the fish swimming against the
current, sometimes staying almost motionless, but always
utterly dependent on the water. For all the anthropomor-
phism of the riddle, it is the fish in its essential nature that
captures the riddler's imagination.

SYMBOLIC ANIMALS

This was not always the case, and the imagination of many
Anglo-Saxons was captivated by the idea of animals doing or
being things which are essentially symbolic. This is related to
the theology of natural revelation, that 'God's invisible qualities – his eternal power and divine nature – have been clearly
seen, being understood from what has been made', as St Paul
puts it in the Epistle to the Romans, 1:20. In other words, creation reflects the nature of God. This takes two particular
directions in Anglo-Saxon literature. Firstly, the natural
world does what is unnatural to show an underlying spiritual

reality, as for example when Balaam's ass speaks to him because it can see what in his spiritual blindness he cannot. And secondly, the natural world images something of spiritual reality when it is allegorically interpreted.

ANIMALS REVEALING SPIRITUAL REALITY

The animal miracle is a favourite type in Irish saints' lives. The anonymous writer of the *Life of St Cuthbert* at Lindisfarne was true to the monastery's Celtic origins when he composed the great Anglo-Saxon saint's life, and there are several animal miracle stories. The best of them is the story of St Cuthbert and the otters:

> Cuthbert was sent for by the nun, widow, and mother of them all in Christ, Aebbe. He came, as invited, to the monastery which is called Coldingham, and staying there some days, did not relax his customary way of life but began to walk about by night on the seashore, keeping up his custom of singing as he kept vigil... That man of God, with resolute mind, approaching the sea went into the waves up to his loin-cloth; and once he was soaked as far as his armpits by the tumultuous and billowing sea. When he came up out of the sea, he prayed, bending his knees on the sandy part of the shore, and immediately two little sea animals followed in his footsteps, humbly prostrating themselves on the earth, licking his feet, rolling upon them, wiping them with their skins and warming them with their breath. After completing this service and ministry, they received his blessing and departed to their familiar place in the waves of

the sea. But the man of God returned home at cockcrow, to join in communal prayer with the brothers in the church of God.

The saint is spied on by one of the brothers of the monastery of Coldingham who afterwards tells the story. And, as is customary, the writer gives a biblical parallel for this miracle: it was, he says, 'just as we read in the Old Testament that the lions served Daniel'.

This story was clearly written by someone who knew how otters behave. The crouching of the animals and their gambolling is interpreted by the writer as humility and kindness. The detail is naturalistic and wholly delightful. But the story signifies much more. Cuthbert has conquered nature in himself and that is reflected in the behaviour of the otters. He has subordinated his own desires, keeping temptation at bay by punishing his body. So when the shy otters serve him, they are acknowledging his conquest of nature.

More than that, they are doing for Cuthbert what he himself had done for an angel. In the chapter before this story, an angel in disguise visited Cuthbert's monastery. Cuthbert washed his hands and feet, drying them with towels, but because of the cold he rubbed the angel's feet with his hands to warm them. So the otters dry Cuthbert with their skins and warm his feet with their breath.

One final detail makes the reference to Daniel understandable. When Bede came to rewrite this story, he omitted both the reference to the otters 'licking [Cuthbert's] feet' and the biblical reference to Daniel. Now in the biblical story, the lions did not exactly 'serve' Daniel, they merely did not eat him. But in Irish sculpture such as the crosses of the Tower at Kells, and Arboe, there are depictions of Daniel in the lions' den which show the lions licking Daniel affectionately. So within the Celtic culture it would be true to say that the otters served Cuthbert as the lions served Daniel. In this miracle of St Cuthbert a new spiritual order takes the place of the old. Nature is transformed by holiness, and the animals recognize and serve the one in whom that holiness is demonstrated.

ANIMALS IMAGING SPIRITUAL TRUTH

Finally, there are creatures, or so the Anglo-Saxons thought, which in their nature image spiritual truth. There is a long tradition of the Bestiary, from Greek, through Latin, to the medieval vernacular languages, in which various animals are understood allegorically. In the Exeter Book of Old English poetry, three creatures are treated in this way: the Panther, the Whale and the Partridge. The last one of these is a fragment, and it is impossible to be sure what it was interpreted to signify. But the other two are perfectly clear. The Whale is an image of the devil, and it has two particular characteristics. It pretends to be an island, so that when sailors moor their ships on it and disembark and light fires, it submerges suddenly and drags them all to their deaths. And it emits a pleasant smell which lures sailors into its mouth, whereupon it gobbles them up. Just so, the poet says, the devil entices people aside from the voyage of good deeds and drags them to destruction; and by the pleasing smell of vain desires, he lures them into the yawning mouth of hell.

The Panther, however, is an image of Christ:

> Throughout the world there are many creatures,
>   innumerable
> species, for the nature of which we cannot
> properly account, nor can we know the number.
> The many multitudes of swarming

animals and birds are as widely spread
throughout the world as this bright undulating
     land
which the water, the raging ocean,
the surging salt waves, surrounds. We have heard
tell about one of these marvellous wild creatures.
It is widely famed among men, it lives
in distant lands and makes its home
in caves in the hills. The animal is called
by the name Panther, as the sons of men,
people known for wisdom, have told us in their
     writings
concerning that lone wanderer. It is a friend
generous with favours to everything but the
     dragon alone:
it lives constantly in extreme hostility with
     the dragon
because of all the evil things that the dragon
     can do.
It is a marvellous animal, incredibly bright
in every colour. Just as heroes,
holy men, say that Joseph's
coat was rippling with colours
of every shade, each one of which shone brighter
and more distinctly than the other
to the sons of men, so this animal's hue,
rippling with every colour brighter and more
     radiant,
shines marvellously so that each one of the colours
is more beautiful, yet more distinct,
and gleams with more glorious splendours,
ever more wonderfully. It has a unique character,
gentle and modest. It is gentle,

loveable and pleasant. It intends to do
no harm to any creature except the venomous
    enemy,
the adversary of old, which I mentioned earlier.
It is always pleased with its food, and when it
    has eaten,
it goes to lie down after its meal
in a secret place in caves under the hills.
There the warrior of the people slumbers
for the space of three nights, occupied with sleep.
Then the courageous one stands up,
roused from sleep, renewed in strength,
on the third day. A melodious noise,
the sweetest of sounds, comes from the mouth of
    the wild creature.
And after the sound, from the place
a scent comes out, an exhalation more pleasant,
sweeter and stronger than any odour
of the flowers of the field or the blossom of
    the trees,
more noble than any of the earth's splendours.
Then from the cities and the royal palaces,
and from the strongholds, many companies of men,
armies of people in troops,
spear-warriors, travel the roadways
driven on by haste. Even animals too,
head into the scent after the voice.
    So it is with the Lord God. The Ruler of all joys
is kind with every favour
to all other creatures except the dragon alone,
the source of poison, the ancient enemy, that is
    to say,
whom he bound in the pit of torments

and fettered with fiery bonds,
covered with punishments.
    And on the third day
the Prince of the angels, the Bestower of victories
arose from the secret place, he who endured death
    for us
for three nights. That was a sweet scent
delightful and pleasant throughout the entire
    world.
Afterwards, righteous people from every quarter
thronged in crowds to that scent
throughout the entire expanse of the earth's
    surface.
As the wise St Paul says,
many are the bountiful good things
throughout the earth that the almighty Father,
the sole Hope of every creature,
whether in heaven or on earth, gives to us as gifts
and for our souls' need. That is a noble scent.

The dragon is 'that ancient serpent who is the devil and Satan' of the book of Revelation, so is naturally the adversary of the Panther or leopard. And so of course the dragon is treated less kindly than the other animals.

    It is clear that the description of the behaviour of both Whale and Panther is as far from naturalistic as it is possible to be. Their behaviour simply represents spiritual truths: the devil is deceitful and murderous, Christ is gentle and loveable. But it is interesting that the animals engage the senses: both are of interesting appearance, and both are associated with scents. The Panther has a melodious voice, too. The intriguing thing is that whereas the poet explains both appearance and scent of the Whale, he does not explain or allegorize these in relation to Christ. So we are left wondering what the scent is. Is it the sacrifice of Christ 'as a fragrant offering ... to God' as in Ephesians 5:2? Or is the scent that of 2 Corinthians 2:14, where God leads Christians 'in triumphal procession in Christ and through [them] spreads everywhere the fragrance of the knowledge of him'? The poet does not tell us. But whereas we know what to avoid in relation to the Whale, we are left with our curiosity and our senses stirred in relation to the Panther. God's image in the animal leaves us wanting to know more.

THE WORLD

The Anglo-Saxons had a robust attitude towards the world: they had to, to survive. It was created by God in beauty, but was a battleground between God and Satan for the souls of humankind. They would not have understood pantheism, the idea that the world itself, and everything in it, is divine. Yet even in the inescapable harshness of life in the real world, the Anglo-Saxons saw that God had left clues about himself in what he had created. They knew that 'the heavens declare the glory of God': the sun and moon, the warmth and glory of light, drew the eye, and raised the spirit to think of higher things. Light so bright it cannot be looked at, imaged the glory of Christ. The animals, too, could teach spiritual lessons, and even image in their mystical nature the truth of Christ. For the Anglo-Saxons, all created things bore the Maker's stamp.

An Old English version of the Benedicite

May the beauty of every skill and deed
in the world praise you, gracious Father.
The heavens and the angels, and the pure waters
which remain above the skies in glory
according to their proper condition, may they
    praise you.
And all created things, the bright heavenly bodies
which keep their courses, the sun and the moon,
each one individually in its order, may they
    worship
you, the Almighty. And the stars of heaven,
dew and fierce shower, may these honour you.
And spirits, mighty God, may they glorify you.
Burning fire and bright summer,
they praise you; night and day together,
every land, light and darkness,
may they praise you in their order, together with
    heat and cold.
And frost and snow, bitter winter weather,
and driving clouds, praise you, mighty Lord
in the skies. And the bright lightnings,
sudden flashes, may these, too, praise you.
All the depths of the earth, the hills and the plains,
the high mountains and the salt sea-waves,
the swelling rivers and the springs of water
welling up, these, too, praise you,
eternal Lord, righteous Creator.
The whales worship you, and the flying birds
of the air; those that stir the waters,
the streams of the sea, and wild animals

and cattle, may these praise you.
And the sons of men love you in their hearts,
and the people of Israel, your servants,
worship you in their proper order, Creator of all
    things.
And the excellences of the hearts of the saints,
the souls and spirits of every righteous one,
praise you, Lord of life, giver of rewards
to all, eternal Lord.
Ananias and Azarias
and Mishael, may they honour you
in the thoughts of their hearts. We worship you,
Lord of all peoples, Father almighty,
true Son of the Creator, Saviour of souls,
Helper of heroes, and Holy Spirit in glory
we praise you, wise Lord.
We worship you, holy Lord,
and in our prayers extol you. You are blessed,
worshipped forever above the roof of the world,
over every land, by the powers of the saints,
high King of heaven and Origin of light.

This hymn, 'O all ye works of the Lord, bless ye the Lord', is
also known as the Song of the Three Children, sung by
Shadrach, Meshach and Abednego in Nebuchadnezzar's furnace, as told in the book of Daniel. This version is from the
Old English poem, *Daniel*.

In the original, the Benedicite is absolutely regular, with
the particular created thing urged, 'bless ye the Lord: praise
him and magnify him for ever'. This imposes order and
regularity on the infinite variety of creation. The Old English
version does what Old English does well, it introduces variety
into the structure. This gives a less controlled, more unpre-
dictable aspect to the world, but it all nevertheless worships
its creator. Even the whale, which as we have seen, had a less
than savoury reputation in the Bestiary, worships God here,
as in the original.

2

MEN AND WOMEN

CLASS

The world of the Anglo-Saxon was a hierarchical one. Broadly we can talk about three classes of people: the slaves, the free, and the noble. Slaves, men or women, were chattels whose rights depended on their owners. The largest class was the free peasants, who had a considerable degree of independence, though they had to pay dues and taxes to the king and services to the local lord. The nobility owned lands, managed estates, held court, ruled monasteries, practised the arts of war, and enjoyed leisure activities like hunting, feasting and drinking, and listening to songs.

THE NOBILITY

The literature naturally tends to concentrate on the nobility and the monastics, since these were the people with the leisure for (or duty of) learning, reading, writing and singing.

But the poet of the Old English *Maxims* gives us a picture

first of the noble life and then of the life and fears of ordinary people.

> A king pays a dowry for a queen
> with goblets and rings. Above all, both must be
> generous with gifts. The skills of war must develop
> in the nobleman, and the noblewoman must grow
> in the affections of her people: she must be
>   even-tempered,
> be able to keep a secret, be open-handed
> with horses and treasures. At the mead-ceremony
> in the presence of the company of warriors, she
>   must always,
> on every occasion, approach first the lord of
>   the princes:
> quickly offer the first goblet
> to the hand of the lord; and she must know the
>   best way
> for them both together to manage the household.

This is a delightful picture of the noble couple. They are both from the upper class, and the marriage is formalized by the exchange of valuables. It might seem that the payment of a dowry of goblets and rings makes this something of a commercial transaction, but the exchange has more subtle meanings. The giving of money in the form of arm-rings symbolizes the value of the woman, who is given by her family to the care of another family. The goblets are treasures of another kind, symbolizing the woman's responsibility to play her part in the social rituals. And if the marriage did not work out, the woman was entitled to have the dowry back when she returned to her family.

The noble couple together rule their household, and both

must be generous. She has her part to play just as he has his. On occasion she has to be discreet, and she has to be wise and cheerful so as to be loved by the people. She also has to fulfil her responsibility for the honour of her lord, paying him public respect and attending first and foremost to him in the mead-ceremony. This passage covers the informal and formal aspects of the noblewoman's role. In *Beowulf* we see the gracious queen of King Hrothgar of the Danes, Queen Wealhtheow, moving among the warriors after Beowulf has killed Grendel, offering the goblet to her lord, giving the hero gifts, and trying to keep everybody not only happy, but well-disposed towards each other. The poet of *Beowulf* hints that it will not work out like that, but not for want of Wealhtheow trying.

ORDINARY FOLK, ORDINARY WORRIES

The *Maxims* poet goes on with another picture of ordinary life.

> When the ship moors,
> the Frisian woman is pleased at the arrival:
> his ship has come back and so has her husband
> returned home,
> her own provider. She ushers him in,
> washes his dirty clothes and gives him clean
> garments,
> allows him on land what his love desires.
> A woman must keep faith with a man.
> Often people accuse women of wickedness.
> Many are faithful. Many are inquisitive,
> and when the husband travels far away, they love
> different men.

The Frisians were the best seafarers of the early Middle Ages. But the women married to Frisian men must have had their fair share of worries. So here we see the woman's relief at the arrival of her husband's ship, and the way she slips into 'busy' mode, bustling about getting her husband washed and properly dressed, and no doubt fed, before sinking into his arms.

The fact that sailors are away for long times at a stretch prompts the poet to muse on morals. The poet does not explore morality in any philosophical way, but simply states that a woman should keep her promise. Irrespective of whether women do or not, scandal gets around. Many women are faithful, but some take the opportunity of their husband's absence to experiment with other men. The way the poet observes what happens takes the heat out of a moral argument which others developed at greater length and with much more vehemence. The point is simply made that promises between men and women should be honoured. And not all scandal is deserved, but plainly some is. The same sort of observation is made earlier in the *Maxims*:

> A girl should properly keep to her embroidery.
> A woman who wanders about gives rise to gossip,
> often people accuse her of wickedness.
> Men say insulting things about her. Often she
>   cannot show her face.

The last part of this is ambiguous: it might mean that the woman's beauty deteriorates. But perhaps the point here is that scandal harms women more than it harms men, and just as the noble woman has to play her part in the social rituals, so also there are socially acceptable roles for freeborn women, which they break only at great risk to themselves.

CHILD-BEARING AND MOTHERHOOD

One of the most important roles for women was child-bearing. This was also recognized as a dangerous thing, and without modern technology and surgery, many women died in childbirth. Archaeological remains of mothers with their child still in the womb have been found. A medical treatise by a man called Bald includes a passage which modern medical practice would endorse:

> A pregnant woman is diligently to beware of eating anything too salty or too sweet or drinking strong alcohol. She should not eat pork or fatty foods; she should not get drunk, nor travel; she should not ride about on horseback too much, in case her child is born before the right time.

A pregnant woman has to take care, and Bald's advice is precisely that: take care. But neither Bald nor the Anglo-Saxons generally could do much when a woman wanted to conceive, or having conceived, could not give birth and the baby was overdue. Charms, mixing common sense and mumbo-jumbo, religion and superstition, ritual and incantation, give these prescriptions:

> If a woman cannot give birth to a child.
> The woman who cannot bring forth her child should walk to the burial mound of a dead man, and climb over the mound three times and say these words three times:

> This to aid me against the hateful
> delayed birth.
> This to aid me against the grievous
> slow birth.
> This to aid me against the hateful
> deformed birth.

And when the woman is pregnant and she goes to her lord in bed, then she should say:

> Up I go, I climb over you
> with a living child not with a dying one,
> with a child to be born full-term, not
> a doomed one.

And when the mother can feel that the child is alive, then she should go to the church and when she comes before the altar she should say:

> To Christ, I said, I have made this known.

The woman who cannot bring forth her child should herself take a bit of her own child's grave and wrap it up in black wool and sell it to merchants, and should then say:

> I sell it, you buy it,
> this black wool and the seed of this sorrow.

The woman who cannot bring forth her child should take the milk of a cow of one colour in her hand and sip it with her mouth, and then go to running water and spit the milk into it. Then with the same hand she should lift up a mouthful of the water and swallow it. She should then say these words:

Everywhere I carried my noble one, the one
    womb-strong,
with this I carried the noble one,
    food-strong,
the one I intend to have and go home
    with me.

When she goes to the stream, she should not look
around at all, nor when she leaves there. Then she
should go into a different house from the one she
left and eat some food.

There is a good deal here that has to do with primitive ani-
mism and sympathetic magic. The first prescription is the
opposite of Bald's advice about resting in pregnancy, and the
active ingredient of the charm is the exercise of the climbing
or walking over the mound, which brings on the labour. But
in folklore, walking over the dead man's grave brings the
overdue baby to life by a principle of opposition; just as climbing over her husband in the next passage transfers his life to
the baby by sympathy. There are doubtless explanations for
the other prescriptions from folklore, but perhaps what is
most evident is the desperation of women who have lost children, their overwhelming desire to have thriving babies, and
the potentially fatal consequences for them if they do not
have a straightforward birth.

We do not often see the domestic happiness of a mother
with her children. Yet one of the riddles collected in the
Exeter Book of Old English poetry shows in a rather sad and
cruel way the kindness of an adoptive mother.

Recently my father and mother
left me for dead. There was no life in me

at that point. Then a very kind woman
covered me with clothing,
protected me and cared for me, wrapped me in a
    protective cover
as kindly as if I were her own child,
until under the fold of her cover, as was
    my destiny,
I came to life among those unrelated to me.
The protective woman fed me after that
until I grew up, and could move about
further on my own. She had fewer of her own
dear sons and daughters for doing this.

The solution to the riddle is, of course, the cuckoo: the cuckoo's egg is laid in another bird's nest, and when the young cuckoo grows it has the habit of ejecting the other nestlings from the nest. What might not be so obvious is the fact that adoption was both a necessity and a social custom among the Anglo-Saxons. Boys particularly were sent away to other families to learn manners and the way of the world. It was by no means impossible that the kindness of the woman who received the child could be ill repaid in the future. Wealhtheow, who has been mentioned already, cared for Hrothulf, her nephew and the man who was to treat his cousins, Wealhtheow's sons, very badly. Wealhtheow might well regret having reared that cuckoo in the nest.

SPIRITUAL MOTHERHOOD

The religious life remained an alternative to marriage and motherhood, or frequently, an option for widows. Abbess Hild was reputed to be the first nun in Northumbria, but it is uncertain whether she was married before this. Her life fell into two equal parts: 33 years as a noblewoman in

Northumbria, and 33 years as a nun and abbess. She was the
niece of King Edwin, the first Christian king of the powerful
northern kingdom. She was commissioned by Bishop Aidan
to set up or establish in a proper fashion the monastery of
Whitby. Bede tells us, echoing Acts 2:44–5, and 4:32–4, that
under Hild's care the community became like the early
Church in its purity and unity:

> no one was rich, no one was needy, because they
> had everything in common and no one thought of
> anything as their own property. Her discretion was
> so great that not only ordinary people looked to her
> for advice and got her help in their difficulties, but
> also sometimes kings and princes. She had those
> who were under her direction spend so much time
> in studying Holy Scripture and doing good deeds,
> that it was easy to find people who were suitable
> for the service of the altar, that is for holy orders.

Hild presided over a double monastery, that is, a foundation
that housed both men and women. Here we see her providing
for her spiritual children, teaching and advising them, and
mapping out a career for them. Five men from Whitby under
her direction became bishops. It was under her rule that
Cædmon developed into a great evangelist by means of his
poetry, nurtured and encouraged and taught by someone who
recognized spiritual gifts as from God, whether the person
receiving them was young or old, noble or commoner.

Bede continues his brief, respectful but affectionate
account of Hild:

> She was not only an example of holy life to every-
> one in her monastery, but she also provided the
> opportunity for salvation and repentance to many

who lived far distant, but who heard the happy news of her reputation for good deeds and virtues. Indeed, Hild, the handmaiden of Christ and abbess, used to be called mother by everyone who knew of her remarkable devotion and grace.

Hild was not a saint in the traditional sense of the word. She had lived the ordinary life of a noblewoman before becoming an abbess. Signs attended her birth and her death, but the miracles she did were not healings or prophecies. They were the minor miracles of using her influence for good, putting aside her own comfort for the benefit of others, devoting herself to caring and encouraging her large 'family'. For this, she was called mother.

There were millions of successful mothers among the Anglo-Saxons. We do not know if Hild was a mother in the normal sense of the word, but undoubtedly she used her gifts as a mother to all at the monastery of Whitby.

'ARMS AND THE MAN'

Most men in the Anglo-Saxon period who were not monks would have had to fight at some time in their lives. Any able-bodied man could be called on to turn out for battle against the Celtic peoples, against other Anglo-Saxons, or against the Vikings. This is a hard fact about life in the Middle Ages and it explains why there is so much in old literature about fighting, loyalty, honour, bravery and death. Different ages responded in different ways to the fact: chivalry in the later Middle Ages was a way of ennobling and idealizing and individualizing the business of fighting and making it serve some romantic and artistic purpose too. Old English literature is closer to the realities, perhaps, but there is still the attempt to transform the blood and guts of war into an ideal, and still the attempt to discern what a Christian might be called to in a society for which battle was a necessity.

The Anglo-Saxons had little doubt that war was not only inevitable but also very often just. It is partly the technology of mass destruction that has undermined that notion for us. But the poet of *Beowulf* makes the issue clear for his audience in two ways: first by making the enemies his hero fights monsters – Grendel and his mother are cannibalistic giants, and the dragon is a fire-breathing destroyer; and second by making the monsters aggressors. So Beowulf fights not humans, about which there was some uneasiness, but monsters, and he fights in defence of people against ravagers, and hence justly.

Beowulf plans to fight Grendel in Hrothgar's hall, as the monster comes to collect his horrible food. In an extravagant gesture of fairness, Beowulf pledges to fight him on Grendel's own terms, without armour or weapons, but relying on his strength and on God:

> I do not consider myself less able in warlike deeds
> and battle-strength than Grendel does himself.
> So I do not want to kill him and deprive him of life
> with a sword, though I perfectly well could.
> He does not know the noble art of war so that he
>   is able to duel with me,
> cutting the shield, though he is famous
> for his deeds of malice. No, in the night
> we must do without swords, if he dares seek
> battle without weapons. And then the wise God,
> the holy Lord, will decree glory
> to whichever of us seems proper to him.

And the poet goes on to say that the hearts of everyone sank.
But

> the Lord granted him
> success in the fortune of battle, granted to the
>   people of the Danes
> comfort and help, so that through the skill of this
>   one man
> and his unaided strength, they all overcame
> their enemy. The truth is evident
> that mighty God has always ruled
> the race of men.

These passages show the skill of the poet at its most subtle.
Beowulf gives his opponent a fair chance, even though his
opponent is a monster. Beowulf boasts as a heroic warrior
should. Heroic ritual prescribed boasting over the mead
before fulfilling the boasts in battle. But Beowulf's boasting is
measured in the sense that he gives place to God's will, and
leaves the outcome in God's hands. It should be remembered
that the poem is set in heathen times, and without knowledge
of Christ, Beowulf behaves in a way that is appropriate for a
Christian warrior, and thus the poet gives an example for his
Christian hearers to follow. Moreover, by Beowulf's battle
with Grendel, he saves the Danes, just as Christ saved his
people by his battle with death and the devil. Truly, the poet
reminds us, God has always been in control.

There is a strong parallel between this fictional situation
in *Beowulf* and the historical battle of Maldon, fought in
991 between Byrhtnoth, the governor of Essex, and a mob of
Vikings intent on raiding the town. A messenger from the
Vikings, who are encamped on the island of Northey in
the tidal River Blackwater, persuasively maintains that the
Vikings will leave the English in peace for a decent payment.

If the English do not pay up, the messenger simply assumes that the Vikings will show them the error of their ways. In true heroic fashion, Byrhtnoth replies that the English will pay swords and spears, but the Vikings will not like it. And in one outright statement, he uses a kind of proverb to boast: 'the heathen must fall in battle'.

Byrhtnoth's army is drawn up on the mainland, and the Vikings on the island try to wade across the causeway separating the two. The English pick them off easily. Then another message comes, possibly some insult or threat which makes Byrhtnoth willing to take a risk. And in an extravagant gesture of fairness like Beowulf's, Byrhtnoth allows the Viking army across the causeway to fight a pitched battle with the English forces:

> Now space has been made for you, come quickly
>   to us,
>   warriors to battle. God alone knows
>   who will be allowed to control the battlefield.

The Vikings, 'wolves eager for slaughter', stream across. Once again the monstrous enemy is given a generous chance by the hero, who leaves the outcome in the hands of God.

Byrhtnoth places himself at the head of his men, and in the battle is soon mortally wounded.

> He was no longer able to stand firm on his feet.
> He looked up towards heaven:
> 'Thank you, Lord of the nations,
>   for all the joys that I have experienced on earth.
> Now, kind Lord, my greatest need is that
>   you grant grace to my spirit,
>   that my soul might be allowed to journey to you,
>   travel in peace into your control,

> Lord of the angels. I beseech you
> that hellish attackers may not be allowed to harm it.'
> Then heathen men hacked him to pieces,
> and both the warriors who stood beside him.
> Ælfnoth and Wulfmær both lay dead
> when they gave their lives beside their lord.

Byrhtnoth prays as the martyrs do, indeed as Christ does on the cross, asking God to receive his spirit, and like Christ, dies with two others. These other two, though not the direct focus of the passage, nevertheless echo Byrhtnoth in their self-giving.

Beowulf and *The Battle of Maldon* are different in many ways. But both poets could appreciate the heroic code of boasting and bravery. Both also show the transformation of the heroic code by Christian values: no longer is the greatest praise for those who kill most, but rather for those who are willing to die for others. What is more, the poets could see how, beneath their extravagance and bravado, warriors were walking in the steps of Christ, putting their lives self-sacrificially at risk in generosity towards the foe, for the sake of the common good.

A century or two ago, all this would have been self-evident to most Christian people. Older hymns are studded with military images:

> Stand up, stand up for Jesus!
> Ye soldiers of the Cross –

and

> Onward! Christian soldiers,
> Marching as to war,

With the Cross of Jesus
Going on before.

In quite rightly shying away from fighting, modern people in
the developed world have perhaps lost some understanding
of the discipline, loyalty and self-sacrifice necessary in the
Christian life.

DUTIES AND WORK

The heroic ideals of the Anglo-Saxons colour most of their
poetry. But we do occasionally get glimpses of what life was
like for ordinary people. A 10th-century code of laws called
Rectitudines singularum personarum sets out, as the title indi-
cates, the rights and duties of different types of people according to their status and roles. It naturally starts with the thane,
the nobleman, who has three primary duties: first to go out
with the army in military service, second to repair the fortifi-
cations in his area, and third to maintain bridges. The code
goes on to deal with many other types of people, for example
the seedsman and the oxherd:

> Concerning the seedsman. It is proper for the
> seedsman to have a full half-bushel of each kind of
> seed, when he has sown each kind of seed well over
> the course of the year.

> Concerning the oxherd. The oxherd is allowed to
> graze two oxen or even more with the lord's herd
> on the common grazing land with the ealdorman's
> [the shire governor's] permission. From these, he
> gets shoes and gloves for himself. And his cow is
> allowed to go with the lord's oxen.

It is clear from these and other laws that the ordinary man and woman had rights in relation to the work they did and the goods they produced. The particular job they did was for an overlord, and was required of them; but the oxherd also had oxen and a cow of his own, and he was entitled to graze them in the same way as the lord's animals. So it was in the oxherd's own interest to do his job well.

Monasteries were major landowners for much of the Middle Ages. Abbot Ælfric devised a dialogue for his school-boys to teach them Latin vocabulary, and the dialogue or *Colloquy* is set on the monastic estate. The boys pretend to be the workers on the estate and have to talk about their work. This is how the dialogue goes:

> *Well, ploughman, what do you say? How do you go about your job?*
> Oh, sir, I have to work hard! I go out at dawn, driving the oxen to the field, and I yoke them to the plough. No winter is so severe that I dare hide at home, because I am afraid of my lord. But when I have yoked the oxen and fastened the ploughshare and the coulter to the plough, each day I have to plough a full acre or more.
>
> *Do you have any companion?*
> I have a boy to drive and goad the oxen. But he is now hoarse because of the cold and from shouting.
>
> *What else do you do in the day?*
> Indeed I do a lot more. I have to fill the mangers of the oxen with hay, I have to water them, and I have to clean out their dung.
>
> *Oh, that is hard work!*
> Sir, it certainly is, because I am not free.

What do you say, shepherd? Do you have to work hard?

Yes, sir, I do. In the early morning I drive my sheep to their pasture and watch over them with the dogs, whether it is hot or cold, in case wolves attack them. Then I take them back to their folds, and I milk them twice a day. I move their folds, and I make cheese and butter. And I am loyal to my lord.

And oxherd, what do you do?

Oh, my lord, I work hard. When the ploughman unyokes the oxen, I lead them to pasture, and all night I watch over them, alert for thieves. And then in the early morning I take them back to the ploughman, well fed and watered.

The dialogue goes on with people in other occupations describing their work: the hunter, the fowler, the merchant, the shoemaker, the salter, the baker, the cook. Of course all of them claim to work hard. But the ploughman has the hardest time, not just because of the demands of the work, unpleasant though they could be. As he says himself, his work is hard because he is not free, he is a slave. And his fear of his master is real. The shepherd on the other hand, though he works hard, is loyal to his lord as a free man. He has rights and duties, he is involved in his work as someone who benefits directly from it.

Now the dialogue takes an interesting turn towards the end. The interviewer asks for some sort of assessment of the importance of the occupations from the estate-manager.

What do you say, wise man? Which occupation seems to you most important?
I say that the service of God seems to me to be most important among the occupations. As it says in the gospel, 'Seek first the kingdom of God and his righteousness, and all these things will be added to you.'

And which of the secular occupations seems to you to hold first place?
Ploughing, because the ploughman feeds us all.

The smith says:

Where does the ploughman get his ploughshare or coulter or goad from, except by my skill? Where does the fisherman get his hook, or the shoemaker his awl, or the sewer his needle? Is it not from what I do?

The estate-manager answers:

It is true what you say, but it is much more pleasant to us all to live with the ploughman than with you. The ploughman gives us bread and drink; what do you give us in your smithy except iron sparks and the noises of beating hammers and blasting bellows?

The manager urges all to work together and to do the work they have before them. Now the ploughman is the only one in the dialogue who is a slave. When the manager puts his work first after the service of God (which is, after all, the purpose of the establishment), he is echoing Matthew 19:30, 'Many who are first will be last, and many who are last will be first', and Luke 9:48, 'he who is least among you all – he is the greatest'. This does not perhaps make the slave's work any easier, but it teaches the boys an important lesson about status.

THE SMITH

The smith takes issue with this judgement on the part of the estate-manager, and so, briefly, does the carpenter. In the light of the evident echo of the biblical passages about status, it is possible that the smith in particular is trying to defend his traditional place of pre-eminence. There were many different kinds of smith, working with different metals and producing various artefacts. The *Colloquy* mentions 'smiths, ironsmiths, a goldsmith, a silversmith and a coppersmith', all on the same estate. Smiths were important people, much valued for their skills. The great legendary smith, Weland, was crippled by King Nithhad to prevent him escaping and taking his skills elsewhere.

The poem *The Gifts of Men* gives examples of two different kinds of smith:

> One is skilful
> with gold and gems when the guardian of warriors
> commands him to set a jewel for his glory.
> Another, an ingenious smith, is able to make
> many a weapon useful in battle,
> when he shapes for the war of warriors
> a helmet or short sword, or chain-mail,
> or a bright sword, or joins the boss
> firmly with a shield to resist the flight of the javelin.

Some of the laws make special provision for the king's smith, and the ability to make suitable weapons for the nobles and warriors conveyed its own status. Doubtless the smith's general line of work meant noise and heat, just as the manager in the *Colloquy* says, but as the smith also says, not much of value could be done without him.

Bede has a dark tale of a smith, whom he knew personally, in his *Ecclesiastical History* which bears this out.

> [The unnamed smith] lived in a noble monastery, but lived an ignoble life. He was frequently reproached by the brothers and elders of the house and urged to live more chastely. But although he would not listen to them, they put up with him for a long time because they needed his secular occupation: he was a remarkably skilled smith. He was much addicted to drunkenness and other pleasures of a wicked life. He much preferred to stay in his smithy day and night rather than go to church to sing the psalms and pray and listen to the word of life with the brothers. It happened to him according to the saying, 'the one who does not wish to enter the church door willingly and humbly, will be made to enter the door of hell unwillingly and damned'.

This man sees a vision of his place in hell and dies miserably. His 'dark mind and dark deeds' mirror the dark place in which he works and foreshadow the dark, hot place to which he will go. But as Bede makes clear, this was not inevitable, but was the result of the man's inability to repent.

THE SMITH AND HIS PATTERN

A much more cheerful view of smithing is found in a curious maxim in a 10th-century Anglo-Saxon manuscript. Someone wrote in a bit of spare space,

> the learned smith must always work according to the pattern or exemplar, unless he is able to do better.

There are all kinds of incongruity about this maxim and its context. Why is a maxim for a smith inserted in a grammatical manuscript? Why is the smith *learned*? Were there many learned smiths? Did a smith write the maxim himself while boning up on his Latin grammar, or did someone else slip it in so that when the smith read it he would not keep designing his own pieces, but actually follow the pattern for once? This maxim certainly needs some unpacking.

The smith here is 'learned'. This might mean a number of things. Certainly it means that he is a monk or cleric. Already we have seen that smiths worked on the monastic estates, and in earlier times particularly smiths could become monks and still practise their craft. In his notes inserted in the Lindisfarne Gospels, Aldred tells us that the covers of the book, sadly now lost, were crafted by Billfrith, a hermit who was a goldsmith. But learned probably also means that the smith knows the traditions associated with metalworking, and that he is a man educated in the teachings of the Church. The writer of this scrap of wisdom does not allow any false distinctions between sacred and secular. A monk must follow his monastery's pattern or Rule of life and worship, and add his own value to it, just as surely as a smith must follow his pattern in making pots or jewellery.

A maxim like this might have applied to the monkish smith in his learning or his craftsmanship. Most medieval religious writers borrow freely from earlier scholars, adding and rephrasing, applying the lessons differently, to new situations. In this they work according to the pattern of the true faith, handed down over the centuries, and add their own understanding to it. Similarly, we might imagine the smith working on a fine piece of jewellery, with a delicate design, or indeed a cooking pot. In these cases, the pattern would give him the dimensions and the basic form and motifs. But if he has richer materials or a better eye than the designer of the original piece, the smith should take the design further, embellish it, enrich it, add to it. The maxim allows the creativity of the individual a place within the patterns and traditions of the work in which he is engaged.

But perhaps most interesting here is something scholars have only recently brought to notice. And here the final piece in the pattern slots into place. The Anglo-Saxons understood and translated the Bible verses that refer to Jesus as 'the carpenter's son' (Matthew 13:55, Mark 6:3) as 'the son of the smith'. As far as the Anglo-Saxons were concerned, Joseph was a smith, a worker of metal, and Jesus was brought up in the trade of the smithy, not the carpenter's workshop. So the monkish metalworker was following, in his life, in his work, in his thought and in his learning, the greatest example of all. He could truly say that whatever he did, he did 'as to God', knowing that he followed the pattern of his Lord.

WOMEN, MEN AND SOCIETY

Modern life is very different from life for the Anglo-Saxons. Medicine has taken huge strides, and makes the prospect of childbirth less fearful than it was, for example. But there are still those who put their lives at risk for the well-being of society as the Anglo-Saxon warriors did. Perhaps one of the most prominent ways that we share the feelings that the Anglo-Saxons expressed is in relation to work. Even today, many people feel that their work is hard and undervalued, some even feel like slaves perhaps. But as we see from the *Colloquy*, even drudgery can be given meaning in a Christian understanding of the world. And like the work of the smith, work can be done according to the pattern of Christ, as duty, as vocation, and as joyful and creative service.

An Old English version of the Lord's Prayer

Our Father who art in heaven.
Father of mankind, help and consolation I pray
    of you,
holy Lord, you who are in heaven.
Hallowed be your name.
May your name now, saviour Christ,
be hallowed in our faithful intellects
firmly established in our hearts.
Your kingdom come.
May your kingdom come to us, to all people,
Lord of power, righteous Judge,
and may glorious faith in you remain in
    our hearts,
all the days of our life.
Your will be done on earth as in heaven.
And may your will among us be fulfilled
in the dwellings of the earthly kingdom,
just as your pure will is in the glory of heaven,
joyfully adorned for evermore.
Give us today our daily bread.
Now give us today, Lord of men,
high King of heaven, our bread
which you sent into the world
for the salvation of our souls –
Christ the pure, that is, Lord God.
And forgive us our sins.
Guardian of men, forgive us our offences and sins
and pardon our crimes, the wounds of the body
and the wicked deeds, with which we often
    anger you,

merciful and almighty God –
As we forgive those who sin against us.
– just as we forgive the crimes which on earth
people often commit against us,
and do not intend to reproach them for their sins,
so that we may merit eternal life.
Lead us not into temptation.
Saviour Christ, do not lead us into misery,
into the pain of sorrow, into temptation,
in case we, hardened against grace through
    enmity,
become estranged from all your mercies.
But deliver us from evil.
And now especially save us from the evil
of every enemy. Lord of the angels,
true Lord of victories, in our hearts
we readily give you thanks and glory
that you in your mercy and by your mighty power
redeemed us from the captivity of hell's torment.
Amen.
Let it be so.

There are several versions of the Lord's Prayer in Old English.
Just as hymn-writers in later times meditated and mused
upon the familiar texts of the liturgy, so did the Anglo-
Saxons. In the version given the poet takes the time-
honoured words and relates them to his own experience. The
prayer that belongs to all Christians becomes personal as the
poet thinks about its words.

The genius of the Lord's Prayer is its focus on giving God
his due first and then asking for him to meet the ordinary
everyday needs of the one praying. Even in giving God his
due, the poet acknowledges his weakness. What he is praying
is true: he knows God is in heaven and is powerful and righteous; he has a sense of the wonder and glory of God and

heaven. But he also knows that the truth about God has to be established in his mind and heart: he needs help to hold on to it, he needs it to enter his being. So he prays not with easy confidence, but with an awareness of his tenuous understanding.

The second part of the prayer focuses on physical and spiritual needs, relationships and conflict. The violence of Anglo-Saxon life is reflected in the prayer for forgiveness, though the phrase 'the wounds of the body' might also mean 'the sins of the flesh'. The poet also gives his own version of Jesus's words in Matthew 6:14–15, 'if you forgive others, your Father will forgive you', when he says 'so that we may merit eternal life'. Forgiveness was not easy for the Anglo-Saxons: vengeance was a pillar of the judicial system and a socially required duty. But the poet's greatest fear is the fear of despair, the weight of misery which crushes faith and undermines a proper sense of the mercies of God. Against evil and enemies, ever-present realities, he can trust the victorious Lord, but this poet is deeply unsure of himself and how sorrow could affect his faith.

The bridge between the two parts of the prayer is made by the request for daily bread. In the original this is the most basic human need for food. But in the Old English version the poet blends the image of an earthly lord providing his warriors with food in return for their loyalty, and the biblical picture of the heavenly Lord who gave the bread of life, his own body, for the life of the world. Thus in a poem which constantly acknowledges the weakness and fallibility of the poet's faith, the writer sets Christ at the centre, as the source of his strength, and the Eucharist as the source of his daily food.

HOME, CHILDREN
AND SONG

The variety and multiplicity of human gifts amazed the Anglo-Saxons. Life itself is a gift from God, to be sure, but the wealth of skills and abilities that human beings have was a source of wonderment. There are several poems in Old English that simply recount the peoples and places where they live, the gifts people have, the pleasures of life – and, because not all of human life is happy, some of the sad ends people come to. The very uncertainty of life in Anglo-Saxon England seems to have given the people a keener sense of the blessings of the moment, and a more resigned and dignified attitude towards inevitable suffering, something we have perhaps lost in our more comfortable society.

HOME AND HOMELESSNESS

The wisdom poems like *The Fortunes* and *The Gifts of Men* and the *Maxims* tend to be fairly detached about what happens in the world. They can talk about good and bad things in much the same way because their role is to observe, not usually to express deep feelings. One of the things several poems comment on is the miseries of the exile, the person who has no friends, home, or social identity, for whatever reason. The *Fortunes* poet puts it like this:

> One man is forced to walk distant roads
> travel on foot carrying his provisions,
> tramping the wet tracks and the dangerous land
> of foreign people. He has no one alive
> to care for him; a friendless man,
> he is hated everywhere because of his bad luck.

The poet of the *Maxims* notes,

> The man who has to live alone is wretched;
> it has been determined that he must remain
>   friendless.
> It would be better for him if he had a brother...

The homeless wanderer was practically an outlaw in Anglo-Saxon times; his legal status was uncertain, and without a family or lord to back him up, he was at the mercy of anyone who wanted to take advantage of him. Because he did not fit into the categories and definitions of normal social life, he was thought to be a threat to others. The similarities between the Anglo-Saxon exile and the modern homeless person are immediately apparent.

But there are several poems in Old English which explore the spirituality of the exile. The speaker in *The Wanderer* seems to be an exile because his lord and his companions are dead. He laments the fact that he has no one to whom he can confide his thoughts. He dreams in the cold misery of half-sleep that he is again enjoying the ordered ritual of loyalty and gift-giving in the hall. But he awakens to find himself in the company only of sea-birds. He sees devastation and loss around him, the snow falling, the night closing in, the winter cold bringing misery.

> All is fraught with hardship in the kingdom of
>   earth;
> change transforms the world under the heavens for
>   worse:
> here wealth is temporary, here friends are
>   temporary,
> here people are temporary, here kinsmen are tem-
>   porary;
> the very foundation of this earth becomes useless.

What possible consolation can there be? Two things give the Wanderer solace. One of these is that he learns wisdom: he sees, with clear sight unblurred by pleasures, the way things are. He yearns for the things he has lost, the horses, the companionship, the feasting and drinking, the rituals of the heroic life; but he sees as never before that they are merely temporary, and a distraction from deeper considerations all too easily forgotten. The other consolation is that he learns to desire what he has experienced almost incidentally in his suffering. He begins with this:

> Often the solitary man experiences grace,
> the mercy of the Lord, though he has long had to
> wander the paths of exile, stir the ice-cold sea
> through the watery ways with his hands,
> anxious in mind.

And he ends with this:

Well it is for the one who seeks grace,
  comfort from the Father in the heavens – where
    for us all security remains.

Deprived of bodily comforts, he learns to seek the grace and comfort of God.

EXCLUSION

The Wanderer is an involuntary exile. So also is the speaker of *The Wife's Lament*. She is an exile because her husband has gone away without her, and left her to the mercy of his family. In her despair she runs away trying to find her lord, or some other friendly face.

First my lord went away from his people
over the tumult of the waves. I had anxious
    mornings
over where in the world my chieftain was.
When I went to find a retinue,
a friendless exile, because of my dire need,
the man's kinsmen began plotting
with dark intent, to separate us;
so that we two have lived as far apart in the world
    as can be,
and have lived most miserably – and I have
    suffered longing.
My lord commanded me to make my home here.
I had no loved one, no loyal friends
in this place, and so my heart is sad.
Then I found the man close to my heart
dogged by misfortune, miserable,
uncommunicative and bloody-minded.

With cheerful demeanour we so often vowed
that nothing would separate us, nothing at all,
but death alone. That is all changed.
Our love is now as if
it had never been. I must suffer, near and far,
the feud of my dearly loved one.

The memory of past joy and its contrast with present misery
fills her with longing and sadness. The slander of her lord's
family has soured their confident relationship with suspicion,
and love has all but died.

Her exile is not an exile of wandering, but of exclusion.
She is forced to live alone, and she thinks of the intimacy of
lovers in the warmth and closeness of their bed. The oppres-
siveness of her surroundings, like the cold that oppresses the
Wanderer, echoes the deep misery of her heart.

I was told to live in a forest grove
under an oak-tree in that earth-cave.
The cave is old, I am overcome with longing,
the valleys are dim, the hills mountainous,
the enclosing hedges sharp, overgrown with
    brambles –
a joyless place. The departure of my lord
often wracks me with pain here. There are lovers
    on earth
living in love, sharing the bed,
when I at daybreak walk alone
round this earth-cave under the oak-tree.
I have to sit there for the days long as summer:
there I can weep over my miseries,
my many sufferings – because I cannot ever
rest from my sorrow,

> nor from all the longing that has come upon me in
> this life.

The only consolation she has is that she is obedient and that she waits, faithfully and painfully, for her beloved:

> Woe it is for one who must
> wait with longing for a loved one.

Small consolation this is. But perhaps when all else fails, finding the resources within to go on, to hope in the face of suffering, is as much as any of us can manage.

EXILE FOR LOVE OF GOD

The theme of exile is given a twist by making it a spiritual discipline. In the Epistle to the Hebrews, the writer points out that Christians 'do not have an enduring city' here; and St Peter in his first letter calls his correspondents 'strangers in the world' and later, 'aliens and strangers in the world'. In the Middle Ages, the practice of *peregrinatio pro amore Dei*, wandering for the love of God, grew up, and this is reflected in the poem called *The Seafarer*. The Seafarer experiences the same hardships and sufferings as the Wanderer: the beating of the sea, the icy chill of the weather, loneliness, dark, and the sense of the transitoriness of all human pleasures. But there is this one difference: the Seafarer willingly undertakes it all because, as he says, 'the joys of the Lord are warmer to me than this dead, transitory life on land'.

Nothing can prepare him for the journey of exile, in which he is wholly dependent on God. Yet it is more compelling than all the heroic pleasures, all the human joys which he leaves behind:

There is no one on earth so confidently brave,
nor so generous in gift-giving, nor so bold in
    his youth,
nor so courageous in his deeds, nor with a lord so
    gracious to him,
but that he has constant fear about his sea-voyage,
as to what the Lord desires to bring him to.
He has no thought for the harp, or accepting
    of rings,
no thought of pleasure in woman, nor hope for
    worldly things,
no thought about anything else other than the
    rolling of the waves.
The one intending to sail has constant anxiety.

The Seafarer finds himself restless and unable to focus on ordinary things. As he thinks about what he is intending to do, his thoughts automatically slip into the heroic mould. In the code of honour by which warriors lived, fame was the most important thing: to be known and to have your story told by the poets was a kind of immortality, even if the deeds by which you brought about fame led to your death. But is that all there is? The Seafarer starts with the merely heroic, but as he thinks about it, he sees that the sacrifice of giving up home and family, joys and comforts, indeed life itself for the sake of God, will bring true immortality. His decision is indeed heroic, but it is also taking seriously the teaching of Jesus in Luke 18:29–30, 'no one who has left home or wife or brother or parents or children for the sake of the kingdom of God will fail to receive many times as much in this age and, in the age to come, eternal life'.

So, the Seafarer decides to fight the spiritual battle and earn spiritual rewards:

For every warrior, therefore, the praise of
    the living,
those who speak of him afterwards, is best.
[This praise] he can bring about before he must
    depart on his way
by noble deeds against the malice of enemies,
by brave actions against the devil,
so that the sons of men praise him thereafter,
and his praise endures among the angels
for ever and ever, in the glory of eternal life,
bliss among the heavenly company.

His experience gives him no immediate pleasure. In fact, like
the Wanderer, he thinks about death, about the way the world
has gone to the dogs, how things have changed for the worse.
One after another the images of decay and death follow themselves unbidden through his mind: 'glory is brought low,
earthly nobility grows old and fragile'. And like glory, so
human beings age and die. Stripped of the social bonds that
give human beings meaning and a place in the created order,
the Wanderer and the Seafarer alike see humankind as the
'poor, bare, fork'd animal' that Shakespeare's King Lear realizes
they are, when he too is stripped of all the trappings of rank
and respect that surrounded him.

But there is a difference between Lear's despair and the
Seafarer's misery. Lear is at the mercy of implacable daughters
and the pitiless elements. But the Seafarer willingly takes on
the elements, the loss and suffering, in obedience to his Lord.
And it is hope that keeps him sane. He ends with determina-
tion, but also the prospect of joy, warmth and intimacy, glory
and love:

Let us think where we have our home
and then consider how we might get there
and then likewise work so that we are able to
    get there,
to the eternal blessedness
where, in the love of the Lord, is the source of life,
hope in the heavens. Thanks be to the holy One
    for this,
that he, Prince of glory and eternal Lord,
has honoured us for all time. Amen.

In his wandering for the love of God, the Seafarer is really journeying home.

HOME AND FAMILY

The Anglo-Saxons gave a lot of thought to the mystery and responsibility of parenthood, as we have seen when we looked at childbirth earlier, and as we shall see below. The poet of *Maxims I* noted,

> Two are mates:
> the woman and the man bring children
> into the world by birth.

Another poet reflected on this in greater depth:

> Very often it happens through the power of God
> that man and woman bring children
> into the world by birth, and they clothe them,
> encourage and love them, until the time comes
> with the passing of years that the young limbs,

vigorous members, reach maturity.
Thus the father and mother carry them and help
   them to walk
clothe them and provide for them. Only God
   knows
what the years will bring as they grow older.

This is the opening passage of the poem before the poet lists some of the unpleasant fates that a person can suffer, such as death in war, blindness, falling out of a tree, exile, the gallows, death by burning, by drunken brawl, even suicide. But then the poet goes on to list the good fortune that people can experience, the happiness they can give, the pleasures they can enjoy. When the children are young, their parents surround them with love and provide everything they need. But the poet faces the fear that every parent knows: children have to grow up, and they cannot be protected from adversity or danger for ever. So, the poet reflects, it is good to remember that birth is God's gift, and the future is in God's hands.

TEACHING CHILDREN

A slightly different issue, beyond clothing, feeding and loving children, is how to bring them up. Abbot Ælfric wrote in the preface to his *Grammar*, 'It is fitting for young people that they learn wisdom, and for the old it is fitting that they teach good sense to their children, because the Christian faith is maintained through teaching.' Ælfric had a good deal of experience teaching children, but as a celibate monk he had no children of his own. Perhaps wisely, he keeps quiet about the practicalities of bringing children up, as distinct from educating them. The poet of the *Maxims* has this to say:

The young man must be taught,
encouraged and persuaded so that he learns well
until he is able to control himself.
He is to be given food and clothes until he is able
    to think for himself.
While still a child he must not be told off before
    he can speak up for himself:
that way, he will flourish to become confident
    in society.
A fierce temper must be restrained.

The focus here is on the child developing independence and becoming confident in social situations. While some things like bad temper merit a degree of severity, much more attention is given to encouragement and nurturing mature attitudes.

Another poem, *Precepts*, shows us what kind of things a father might have had to say to his son. The poem lists ten precepts, and is clearly modelled on the Ten Commandments in this. Here is the first instruction:

Always do what is good and your deeds will
    be worthwhile.
God will always be your Lord and helper
in every good thing; the devil will be lord
    and helper
to others in more evil deeds. Look for the better,
and carry this out with courage as long as you live.
Love your father and mother with your heart,
and each one of your family, if they love God.
Always be courteous to your elders
and dutiful, and keep your teachers
in your heart, kindly in mind:
they encourage you most eagerly in goodness.

The father goes on with good advice: don't get involved in bad behaviour, choose your friends carefully, don't let your friends down, don't get drunk and sleep around, try and make a clear distinction between good and evil, keep your own counsel, learn all you can, follow the scriptures, keep your self-control in word and deed. No doubt in the modern world we wrap things up differently, but this is the way of living we too generally wish for children. And while the resemblance to the Ten Commandments is principally due to the number of separate instructions the father gives, nevertheless it is clear that the instructions are made up of a tissue of biblical quotations: 'Love your father and mother' here takes the commandment and expands it as St Paul does in Ephesians 6:1–2, 'Children obey your parents in the Lord ... honour your father and mother'.

LOSS

The death of children is one of the most distressing things human beings can face, and it is one the Anglo-Saxons faced frequently. In *Beowulf*, the old king Hrethel has to live with the fact that his son, Herebeald, accidentally killed his own brother Hæthcyn when they were out hunting. Hrethel pines because the usual recourse of vengeance is impossible, and no legal redress is available against his own son. He is like a man whose son is executed by hanging.

> It is a miserable thing for an old man
> to experience, that his young son
> should swing on the gallows. He recites a poem,
> a sorrowful lament, when his son hangs
> for the benefit only of the raven, and he as an old
>   and wise man

can do absolutely nothing to help him.
He is regularly, every morning, reminded
of his son's passing. He cannot care
to wait for other heirs to come
into the dwellings, when this one
has met with deeds resulting in death.
He looks with grief in his son's room,
the deserted hall, the bed occupied only by
    the wind,
bereft of joy – the riders, heroes,
sleep in the grave. There is no sound of the
    harp there,
no joy in the dwellings, as once there was.
He goes to bed then, sings a song of sorrow,
one man for one man. The lands and houses
seemed to him far too spacious.

The old man would be someone to whom people turned in their trouble. But all his wisdom is useless, and he is confronted by the complete helplessness we all feel before death. Nothing can be done. And he is endlessly reminded of his son by ordinary things, which recall unbidden the joys of the past and renew the grief: the silent room, the empty bed, the unbearable sense of vacant space where there should be life and laughter.

It is perhaps this sense of the preciousness of children which leads one poet to change the words of scripture. The ending of Psalm 137 is brutal, when it suggests the Babylonian conquerors of Jerusalem deserve no less than what they have done to the Israelites: 'happy is he who repays you for what you have done to us – he who seizes your infants and dashes them against the rocks'. The Anglo-Saxon poet turns this utterly on its head:

Blessed is he who takes and sets
his own son on that noble rock.

The Babylonian children become one's own children, and
instead of harming them, the poet urges that they should be
established and built upon the noble Rock, Christ himself.
And so the lesson of loss is learned, children are cherished and
brought up with their lives based on the foundation of Christ.

SONG

The new version of Psalm 137 might have been sung with
more gusto than the original one, even by the hardened warrior. The monastic life was ordered around the singing of the
psalms, and the popularity of the psalter is no doubt a reflec-
tion of the popularity of songs more generally. For it is clear
that the Anglo-Saxons loved songs. Secular songs were more
than just words and music, though of course they were words
sung to the harp. Songs usually meant joy and togetherness,
feasting and drinking, and even sad songs could contribute to
the joy. In *Beowulf*, the celebrations following the hero's victory over the monster Grendel include drinking and singing:

There was song and music both together
in the presence of the battle-leader of Healfdene's
    line;
the harp was played, many a story told,
when Hrothgar's poet had to relate
for entertainment among the mead-benches
the story of Finn's people, how disaster befell
the hero of the Danes, Hnæf of the Scyldings,
on the Frisian battle-field, and how he had to die.

The story that follows is one of the most bloodthirsty and terrible tales of vengeance to be found in Old English. But the story was one in which the Danes won a victory over the treachery of the Frisians and Jutes, and the song stirs the minds of Hrothgar's people to remember their heroic past.

The occasion for singing was nearly always a communal one. The Anglo-Saxons did not have the technology for listening to music and song on their own. Moreover, no matter how personal the song (and we have seen just how deeply personal some of the songs are), it had a singer and an audience, it celebrated the values of the community, it reminded people of their past and it gave them a sense of belonging, a place in the tradition.

One of the happy things that can happen to a man in *The Fortunes of Men* is that he becomes a singer.

> One man is able to delight a group of warriors,
> make the men drinking on the benches round the
>   hall happy.
> That is a great joy to the drinkers there.
> Another sits at his lord's feet
> with his harp and is given money,
> he constantly, rapidly, caresses the strings,
> makes the leaping plectrum, the plucking nail,
> sound out the music. He is utterly rapt.

The last phrase is difficult to translate: it could mean something like 'it is an important duty to him', or as one scholar has translated it, 'he shows great verve'. But the heathen Anglo-Saxons thought that poets were inspired by the gods, and the Christian Anglo-Saxons certainly saw poetry as a special gift from God. So it seems possible that the need or compulsion the poet has to tell his story, and the concentration he has on the music is what is referred to.

A RELUCTANT SINGER

The story of Cædmon, told by Bede and much loved by the Anglo-Saxons, records how one man was given a gift of poetry from God. This gift not only transformed the Anglo-Saxon poetic tradition by giving it words to express its new Christian faith, but also gave the people a new Christian history in which they had their place. The story translated from the Old English version of Bede's *Ecclesiastical History* is this:

> In Abbess Hild's monastery [at Whitby] there was a certain brother singularly honoured and dignified by a divine gift, in that he habitually composed suitable songs which related to religion and piety. So that, whatever he learned from religious writings through scholars, the same he produced after a space of time in verse of the greatest sweetness and inspirational quality in well-turned English. And through his songs, the minds of many were often kindled with contempt for the world and desire to join the spiritual life. Many others after him in England began to compose religious songs, but none could do it quite like him, because it was 'not from man nor by human means' that he learned the art of poetry, but he was divinely helped and received the art by the gift of God. Because of that, he never composed songs of fiction or idle pleasure, but only such as related to piety was it appropriate for his pious tongue to sing.
>
> This man was established in secular life until he had reached advanced age and he never learned any songs. Because of this, whenever it was decided that there should be a party and that they should

all sing in turn to the harp, he often got up in shame from the feast and went home. On one particular occasion he did this, that is, left the house where the party was, and went out to the cattle shed where it was his responsibility to look after the animals for the night. Then when he lay down to rest at the appropriate time and slept, a certain man appeared to him in a dream, and addressed and greeted him, and called him by his name, 'Cædmon, sing me something.' He answered and said, 'I don't know how to sing anything, and for that very reason, I went out of tonight's party and came here, because I do not know how to sing anything.' The one who was speaking to Cædmon said again, 'But you are able to sing to me.' So Cædmon said, 'What must I sing?' He said, 'Sing me the creation.' When he got this answer, he immediately started to sing in praise of God, words and verses that he had never heard, and this is their sequence:

Now we ought to praise the Guardian of the
    kingdom of heaven,
the might of the Creator and his understanding,
the works of the Father of glory, how he, the eternal
    Lord
established a beginning of each wonder.
He, the holy Creator, first created
heaven as a roof for the sons of the earth.
Then the Guardian of humankind, the
    eternal Lord,
the almighty Prince, afterwards created
the world, the land for the people.

Then he got up from his sleep and all the things he had sung in his sleep he retained firmly in his memory, and quickly to those words he added more words in the same style, of songs dear to God. He went in the morning to the reeve who was his master and told him the sort of gift he had received. He took him immediately to the abbess, and told it to her. She commanded all the most learned men and the teachers to assemble, and commanded him to tell the dream and sing the song in their presence. Then the judgement of all, as to what the gift was and where it had come from, was sought. They all said (which was actually the case) that a spiritual gift had been given to Cædmon by God himself. Then they read out a holy story and told him some words of spiritual instruction, asking him, if he was able, to change these into delightful verse. When he had received this material he went home to his house and came back in the morning, and giving them back what they had given him, sang the best decorated verse.

The abbess embraced and praised the gift of God in the man, and she urged and instructed him that he should leave his secular life, and become a monk, and he readily accepted that. She received him and his goods into the monastery and inducted him into the community of God's servants. She commanded him to be taught the whole course of sacred history and scripture, and he, retaining in his memory all the things that he could learn from listening, like an animal chewing the cud, transformed them into the sweetest verse. And his song and verse were so delightful to hear, that his very teachers wrote down what he said and learned it.

He sang first of all about the creation of the world and the origin of humankind and the history of Genesis (the first book of Moses); next about the exodus of the Israelite people out of the land of Egypt and afterwards the entry into the Promised Land; and about many other accounts in the canonical books of Holy Scripture. And about Christ's incarnation and his suffering, and his ascension into the heavens, and the coming of the Holy Spirit, and the teaching of the apostles. And next he composed many songs about the future Day of Judgement and about the fearfulness of the torments of hell and the sweetness of the heavenly kingdom. And likewise he composed many others about the divine judgements and blessings. In all these he diligently took care to draw people away from love of sin and evil deeds and to incite in them love and desire for good deeds. For he was a very pious man, humbly devoted to the discipline of the monastic rule, and he became zealously incensed with those who wished to act otherwise.

Cædmon's misery is that he cannot sing and join in with the others, and this makes him an outsider, a little like an exile. He leaves the party and keeps the company of animals. Perhaps it is appropriate for a herdsman that when he is given his gift, he becomes like the cow chewing the cud and turns ordinary things into wholesome and useful nourishment for the soul. The gift not only turns his life upside down, but adds a new dimension to poetry and the pleasure it gives. Bede, who must have known Cædmon's poetry if the Old English translator is right that some of it was written down, is full of praise for its beauty and dignity. Moreover, the pleasure it gave reinforced the message: this was not just poetry telling a good story in a good style, but it was poetry which communicated the truth in a way that moved and stirred, delighted and challenged people. The great hymn-writers over the centuries have always attempted this, and the English writers follow in Cædmon's footsteps.

DEEP FEELINGS AND SONG

The poet of the *Maxims* neatly expresses the complex of feelings surrounding songs:

> Wise words are appropriate for every man,
> songs for a musician, and discretion for a
>   nobleman.
> There are as many views as there are people on
>   earth:
> everyone has their own perspective.
> He has less anxious yearning who knows many
>   songs,
> or can play the harp with his hands:
> he has the gift of music which God gave him.

Wise words and songs are spoken and sung by individuals, but nevertheless express what the community believes. But the poet knows that if people were asked their opinions about almost anything, there would be as many views as there are people. The Roman poet Terence said as much in the proverb, *Quot homines, tot sententiae*, 'many men, many minds', and the *Maxims* poet is echoing that proverb here. But he returns to the things that unite even the most disparate minds: the simple pleasures of song. He also hints at another function of poetry and song, namely the way it can take people out of themselves and give them a way of expressing anxiety, sorrow, misery, all kinds of negative emotion, without hurting others. The anxiety of the individual can be made into art, which is a gift of God.

In the obituaries columns of the local newspapers we find this art.

Time will not dim the face we love,
The voice we heard each day,
The many things you did for us
In your own loving way.
We hold you close within our hearts
And there you will remain,
To walk with us throughout our lives
Until we meet again.

Or another,

Someone special, good and kind,
Treasured memories left behind.
Our wish today is just a prayer,
God bless and keep you in his care.

Prose cannot quite express the deepest of our feelings. People need something both formal and intimate in times of trouble, such as when they are bereaved. Verse imposes order through rhyme and rhythm, but yet allows people to say things that they might find embarrassing, or disturbing, or too painful if they were in prose. It even allows people to talk about God without sounding sanctimonious. Earlier we saw that the old man whose son was hanged sang his sorrow. So we can

understand the Anglo-Saxon poet's view that poetry somehow helps people in their difficulties.

One of the most touching laments in Old English is the
poem *Deor*. Deor, whose name means 'dear, beloved', tells the
story of his own little bereavement, the loss of his job.

> The person deprived of joys sits anxious,
> and his mind becomes gloomy. It seems to him
> that his share of sorrows might be limitless.
> At this point he might consider that throughout
>   this world
> the wise Lord frequently brings changes:
> to many a noble man he shows favour,
> brings assured prosperity; to others a share
>   of miseries.
>
> I want to say one thing about myself.
> It is that for a time I was the court poet of
>   the Heodenings,
> I was dear to my lord, and my name was 'Dear'.
> For many years I had a good job
> and a gracious lord; until now, when Heorrenda –
> a very skilful musician – has taken over the estate
> that the lord of the warriors once gave to me.
> Other sorrows passed: so may this.

Before this, Deor has given examples of suffering from
Germanic legend, including the torture of Weland the smith
by King Nithhad, Weland's vengeance on the king including
the rape of Beaduhild, Nithhad's daughter, and the murder of
Nithhad's sons. And after each one (uniquely in Anglo-
Saxon poetry) he gives the refrain, 'that sorrow passed: so may
this'.

Then, as the extract above starts, he imagines 'someone' who might be suffering, and says something like Job's 'The Lord gave and the Lord has taken away' (Job 1:21). Here the refrain is missing, because the argument is a theological one: it is all – pain and pleasure, suffering and joy – in God's power, and he can change it as he wills. This is of course true. But as C.S. Lewis once wrote, 'don't come talking to me about the consolations of religion or I shall suspect that you don't understand'. Our poet can find no direct consolation for his misery from his faith. He can see rationally that everything is within God's providence, but it does not ease the pain. The fact that some people are happy hardly makes it easier when he is sad.

So he reluctantly comes to the point of his song, his own suffering. He has been sacked from a good job, and another man has taken job, pay and prospects from him. He generously acknowledges the other man's talent, and the kindness of his lord over the years. But now all he can hope for is that time, as in the case of Weland and the others, will bring relief and numb the pain. Other sorrows passed, perhaps this one will, too. What he has done is to use his God-given gift of poetry to express his suffering. Even though he has a job as a poet no longer, he turns to poetry. And it is through his poetry that we can understand his anguish and his consolation.

HOME, CHILDREN AND SONG

It is said that 'absence makes the heart grow fonder'. Old English poems often celebrate those things like home and family and song, which in their absence make for the greatest sadness. It is a mark of the strength of their faith, that some Anglo-Saxons could willingly give up home and family for the sake of a spiritual home and a spiritual family. And it is a mark of the resilience of their faith that they could sing, even of loss and grief, and in the singing find a small measure of consolation. Song is a gift imparted to others, an affirmation of meaning in life, a gift of God.

An Old English meditation on singularity

Rejoice now in your heart, and take your Lord
as a solace, and raise up glory for yourself;
keep your own counsel, bind up your thoughts
within your heart. Many things are unknown,
trusty companions sometimes fail,
and promises become weak. That is the way this
    world goes,
it rushes on with showers of rain and runs to its
    fated end.
Faith is one, the living God is one,
baptism is one, the eternal Father is one,
the Creator of people is one, who made the earth,
good things and joys. Glory grew thereafter,
though for a long time this passing creation stood,
hidden in darkness, concealed under a cover,
well screened by trees, smothered by gloom,
when a young woman
grew up brave among humanity
in whose treasured body it pleased the Holy Spirit,
    the Creator of life, to be.
Bright on her breast shone the radiant child,
who was the Origin of all light.

This poem is called *Homiletic Fragment II* by the editors of the
Exeter Book of Old English poetry, where it is found. But
there is no indication in the manuscript that it is a fragment.
In fact, it is a meditation on different kinds of aloneness, sin-
gleness, uniqueness. This is the 'singularity' which threads
through the poem and makes it a unity.

The poet starts with the exile theme, and the third line echoes almost exactly a line from *The Wanderer*. What can a person do when he or she feels let down and completely alone? The poet counsels trust in the Lord, and not complaint. But that willingness to trust in the Lord is also an answer itself, because by trusting one becomes part of a much greater whole, the community of faith. The poet paraphrases Ephesians 4:5–6, 'One Lord, one faith, one baptism; one God and Father of all, who is over all and through all and in all', emphasizing that the believer becomes part of that unity which is God's creation through Christ. But the creation had to wait for a long time in the gloom before the coming of the true Light, just as a lonely person feels the gloom of separation from the joy of being with others. But then uniquely by the Holy Spirit, to a unique young woman, Mary, the unique source and origin of light, Christ the Light of the world, came into the world.

To be alone for this poet is to share a much wider experience: it means to share in the mystical unity of the Church, to become one with creation which waits in longing for its redemption, and to reflect the unique Light of the world. The poet explores the paradox by which loneliness makes the Christian a participant in mystical communities.

4

WISDOM

Most poetry in Old English is aristocratic. It reflects the ideals of the upper class, the warriors and noblemen and women who had leisure for this kind of entertainment and could employ poets. Or it is learned, the product of monks and nuns, people who had access to education and Latin learning. Part of the miracle of Cædmon's gift of song was that Cædmon was obviously a man of the lowest class, a mere herdsman, and yet he produced songs that taught his social betters religious truth. He was an object lesson in the biblical principle that the humble shall be exalted. Sadly only nine lines of verse survive that can with any certainty be ascribed to Cædmon, so we have no means of telling whether all of his verse was in the same style as his famous *Hymn* or not.

COLLECTIONS

But there are several collections of proverbial and educational material that seem to be popular, speaking the language of the man in the field and the woman at her needlework. These collections are often earthy in expression and quirky in

content. They are very similar to the biblical wisdom books
of Proverbs and Ecclesiastes, and to the apocryphal books of
Wisdom and Ecclesiasticus or Sirach. They are concerned with
practical wisdom, behaving properly in the world, and also
with what can and cannot be known about the world.
Sometimes they seem like miscellaneous observations, lists
of curiously unconnected aphorisms. But sometimes they are
given a framework, or put together in a thread which makes
sparks fly; and sometimes just a phrase or two will strike home,
with a shock of recognition, as profoundly or strangely true.

Wisdom is a category for which the modern world has little
use. We prefer scientific, preferably technological knowledge,
which allows us to manipulate our world and use its resources
for our benefit or comfort. Before the scientific revolution of
the 18th century, wisdom embraced two kinds of knowledge.
On the one hand it comprised the sort of empirical, observa-
tional information that became science, and on the other it
included the practical, dutiful, religious understanding of life
that came with age and experience, and that parents taught
to their children – a tradition in which people lived. The
sages were usually old, and were widely respected for their
experience: an Old English word for 'wise', 'a wise person', is
frod, and it means 'old, experienced' as much as it means
'wise'. As Job says, 'Is not wisdom found among the aged?
Does not long life bring understanding?' (Job 12:12).

The wisdom of the sages was not particularly their own,
though they might add to the common stock, but it consisted
of what everybody could in principle know. The individual is
not so important in wisdom as the people. One of the Old
English wisdom poems says 'wise men must exchange sayings',
and so they did. Anglo-Saxon wisdom borrows from many
different sources: the Bible and learned literature, folklore,
history and other kinds of tradition. It became custom to

attribute wisdom to characters such as Solomon and King Alfred, but some sayings originated in the experience of ordinary people and others were borrowed.

PRACTICALITY

Wisdom is not just knowing things. It is about doing and being, too. One of the wisdom poems asserts the communal value of wise people and their activities:

> One wise man
> holds a meeting with another: their minds
>   are similar.
> They always resolve disputes and teach peace
> which unfortunate people have disrupted earlier.
> Counsel belongs with wisdom, justice with
>   the wise,
> a good man belongs among good men.

In one of King Edmund's laws, he makes provision for resolution of disputes by saying that 'Wise men must settle feuds.' The wise mediate between people. In law they have more specific functions, but most often the laws make binding what earlier custom practised. And Old English law was not forensic in the modern sense, so there was need for wisdom in maintaining law and order. Anglo-Saxon wisdom, then, is about knowledge, experience, community and practicality. But as we shall see, it is not without humour or colour.

THE DURHAM PROVERBS

A collection of proverbs is found in a manuscript of the 11th century in Durham Cathedral Library. The *Durham Proverbs* include various sayings about friends ('No one can have too many friends'), the value of moderation ('No one should be too easily frightened or too easily pleased'), about words and deeds, about relationships between people. Some of these are biblical, or similar to biblical sayings: 'All that is in the mind is in the mouth' compares with 'out of the overflow of the heart the mouth speaks' from Matthew 12:34 and elsewhere; and 'Need tests friends', an early version of 'A friend in need is a friend indeed', compares with 'A friend loves at all times' from Proverbs 17:17. Another proverb, 'If you speak well, do as you say', is probably to be related to the parable in Matthew 21:28–32, about the two sons who were asked by their father to work in his vineyard, of whom the one who refused did work and the one who promised to work did not. And it appears to relate, too, to a passage later in Matthew, where Jesus warns against the Pharisees who do not practise what they preach (in the Latin Bible, Matthew 23:3, 'they say and do not do').

There is often a sense of incongruity, something odd, about wisdom collections. Two manuscripts were bound together in the volume which contains the *Durham Proverbs*: the first part is an important book of Latin hymns and canticles, with Old English glosses; and the second part is a version of Ælfric's *Grammar*. The proverbs are written in between the hymns and the canticles, and they have Latin versions accompanying them. For various reasons, the Latin is thought to be translating the Old English rather than the other way about. But apart from the fact that the hymns and the proverbs have both Latin and Old English versions, the connections between the wisdom literature and the rest of the manuscripts are not always obvious. It takes quite a bit of ingenuity to see what connection there might be between the dignified Latin hymns and canticles and the rather earthy proverbs. But there can be little doubt of the value that the Anglo-Saxons attached to the proverbs, simply from looking at where they are written.

Some of the *Durham Proverbs* are the earliest English examples of a proverb type known as the Wellerism because of its frequent use by the loquacious and humorous Sam Weller in Dickens's *Pickwick Papers*. This type of proverb must have been intended as funny. For example:

'Now it's up to the pig,' said the peasant astride the boar's back.

'Nevertheless I wouldn't trust you, though you go well,' said the man who saw a witch going along on her head.

'Bigger is not better,' said the man who heard wailing in hell.

'Whoever wants you can have you,' said the man who saw famine leaving the town.

It is not always easy even to understand what the proverbs mean. Possibly the one about the pig means that once you give over control of life or possessions to someone or something else, you depend on them rather than on yourself. The next two are more obvious and say similar things: just because someone can do something impressive, it does not mean they can be relied on for everything; and of course in relation to some things like wailing and hell, unimpressiveness is much the better part. The last of the Wellerisms quoted is similar to a passage from the wisdom poem already quoted, known as *Maxims I*:

> The ordaining Lord alone knows
> where the plague goes, that departs from our land.
> He adds children where early death takes away,
> so that there are just as many people on earth;
> there would be no limit to the population
> if he who made the world did not diminish it.

Here, though, the departure of the plague gives rise to sombre reflections about death and birth, the continuance of the human race and the providence of God.

A WORLD VIEW

These proverbs tell us a great deal about the way the Anglo-Saxons viewed their world. There is hardship and death, strife and deception. 'A guilty man needs refuge' suggests some of the horrors of the system of vengeance that Anglo-Saxon society was based upon. But there is humour, and it breaks out in vivid images. 'It will be a good year when the dog gives to the raven', notes one proverb. When scavengers have enough to share with each other, it certainly will be a good year: but then, pigs might fly. 'You can't have a mouth full of flour and also blow a fire' notes another proverb: don't try to do two things at once. 'He does not know the pleasure of the sweet who has never tasted the bitter' is echoed by a similar proverb in the Old English *Rune Poem*, 'he does not enjoy hope who knows little sorrow', and an exhortation in the Old English *Dicts of Cato*, a proverb collection translated and modified from a Latin source, attributed to the Cato of the title:

> Always balance joy and sadness; because if one of
> them is any greater than the other then there will
> be an unbalance, and you will only with difficulty

be able to face the things that happen to you;
because neither of them can be perfect without the
other, any more than wet can exist without dry, or
warm without cold, or light without darkness.

So the recommendation is to take the rough with the smooth,
perhaps, and enjoy the smooth while you have it.

The earthiness and vividness and humour of these proverbs
shows their popular origin. But they were valued no less
because they were popular. The very incongruity of the
proverbs in this manuscript shows how significant the Anglo-
Saxons thought wisdom to be. It was worth preserving even
in an important liturgical manuscript. It is curious that
another small group of verse proverbs was preserved twice
in similar contexts. The proverbs, given in Latin and Old
English in both manuscripts, read:

Heat grows cold, white becomes dirty,
the beloved becomes hated, light becomes dark.
Everything which is not eternal decays with age.

In one manuscript, containing Ælfric's *Grammar* and *Glossary*
and the *Benedictine Rule*, the verse is preceded by a prose
proverb, 'The apple never rolls so far that it does not know
where it came from.' And in the other manuscript, containing
a psalter, the verse is preceded by two of the proverbs which
appear in the Durham collection, 'Better often loaded than
overloaded', and 'Everyone who calls desires a response.'
Once again the value of the proverbs is proved by the fact
that they are preserved where they are. And the accompanying proverbs perhaps take some of the sting out of the view of
life expressed in the verse, that everything gets worse or grows
old: warmth, purity, love, light and youth, do not last. No

doubt this is substantially true, but it is also substantially depressing.

The Christian content of these proverbs is not always obvious. We have seen that some of them derive from the Bible. Others take for granted a Christian world view that encompasses eternity and hell. The one consolation offered by the verse proverbs just mentioned is the fact that they admit some things as eternal, though they do not specify what those things might be. The similarity between these proverbs and Henry Francis Lyte's famous hymn, 'Abide with me', could easily be missed:

> Swift to its close ebbs out life's little day;
> Earth's joys grow dim, its glories pass away;
> Change and decay in all around I see:
> O Thou who changest not, abide with me!

NOT ALL PROVERBS ARE TRUE

Although proverbs were valued among the Anglo-Saxons, they were not always orthodox, or appreciated by the powers that be. In a society without wide access to books, proverbs could be, and were, quoted as authorities without deference to the Bible and Christian teaching. Archbishop Wulfstan shows this happening in one of his sermons:

> Antichrist and great liars say as a proverb that 'he is sharpest and wisest of mind who can most readily contrive and most often deprive the unwary of something'. The foolish also say as a proverb that 'great asceticism is of little importance', but that 'food was made for the sole purpose that people

should eat it, and woman for the purpose of sexual
intercourse for those who desire it'.

Wulfstan quotes these as proverbs, and they may have been
genuinely popular. The last proverb certainly has 16th-
century and later parallels, 'All meats to be eaten, and all
maids to be wed'. The Old English word for food is *mete*,
which makes the parallel even clearer. In another chapter, we
see the social chaos in which Wulfstan was living, and plainly
he views the opportunistic, every-man-for-himself, look-after-
number-one, do-as-you-please emphasis of these proverbs as
a symptom of social decline. Moreover, the second two
proverbs attack the very basis of the great movement for
monastic reform that had given peace and stability to English
life in the mid-10th century: Benedictine monasticism valued
asceticism, abstinence from bodily pleasures, and did not
allow monks to eat meat at all in normal circumstances. So
Wulfstan attributes these proverbs to Antichrist himself.
    He goes on to say,

> But the truth is, as I say, that by means of all such
> teachings, Antichrist entices and hatefully leads
> astray all too many. For never in the world is there
> any worse law than that someone should entirely
> indulge his inclination, and set his own inclination
> up as law for himself ... But he is blessed who
> examines himself to any degree.

Wulfstan acknowledges the persuasiveness of such popular
proverbs, and the tendency for them to become, in the popular mind, guides to action, rules of thumb. But he wants to
warn people not just to hear the sound of authority in the
proverbs, so as to use them mindlessly, but to assess what they

say. And clearly he recommends people to give a different kind of attention to themselves from that recommended in the proverbs. They should not look to satisfy their inclinations, but should rigorously examine their motives. This sense that proverbs might be at variance with truth, religion and propriety has a long history from here on: many later writers regarded proverbs as common and undignified. In the 18th century, Lord Chesterfield famously wrote to his son that 'a man of fashion never has recourse to proverbs'.

THE FEAR OF THE LORD IS THE BEGINNING OF WISDOM

For all the apparent vagueness of the Christian content of the wisdom literature, neither people, nor poets, nor scribes were in much doubt that 'the fear of the Lord is the beginning of wisdom'. This is made explicit in *Maxims I*, which after a line or two asking for the hearer to engage in wise discussion with the speaker, continues with:

> First of all, God our Father must
> fittingly be praised, because he ordained life and
>   passing pleasures
> for us at the very beginning: he wishes to remind
>   us of those gifts.
> The Lord dwells in glory, the young person
> on earth grows old. God is eternal to us:
> nothing that happens changes him, and nothing,
> neither disease nor age, afflicts the Almighty at all.
> He does not grow old in spirit, but he is even now
>   as he was before,
> the patient Lord. He gives us minds,

various dispositions, many languages.
Far and wide, many an island
embraces all kinds of living things. The Lord,
   Almighty God,
created spacious homelands
for humankind, and as many of both things –
peoples and customs.

This passage takes up the concern of the proverbs with the process of decay but it emphasizes the difference between God and all created things. The poet works with a biblical pattern from James 1:17–18, which makes it clear that God 'does not change like shifting shadows'. But though God is different from people, he is not indifferent to people. All the rich variety of life, all the bewildering range of pleasures, peoples, places, customs and dispositions, show his creativity and generosity. So although pleasures are transitory, life is complex and variety in creation is endless, these things are gifts from God, and the response of wisdom is to praise him.

CHARACTERISTICS AND STRUCTURE

This poem then continues to look around at the world and to list the characteristics of things. This is typical of ancient wisdom literature. It looks at things in their characteristic forms, and expresses a generic world view: in other words, we are dealing with 'everyone' or typical parents, typical children, typical teachers, with the wise or foolish, with brave or idle or talkative people, with friends and enemies, kings and slaves, the godly and the godless. Or we are dealing with the characteristics of categories of things like the seasons, or the place of creatures like wolves, boars, bears, salmon. Because even a generic world view is bewilderingly miscellaneous in its actual outworking, the wisdom collections impose structure. Nearly all of them are in verse, because verse is structured, and this is one way of mentally controlling the infinite variety of things. It puts things in an ordered, disciplined system.

In the poem called *Maxims II* there are several themed catalogues. After a nod in the direction of kings and cities, the poet enters upon a list of things that are superlative, 'the swiftest', 'the most powerful', 'the brightest' and so on:

> Wind in the sky is swiftest,
> thunder is loudest at times, the powers of Christ
>   are great.
> Fate is most powerful, winter is coldest,
> spring is frostiest and cold for the longest time,
> summer is brightest with sun, the air is hottest,
> autumn is most glorious and brings to noblemen
> the year's fruits which God sends to them.
> Truth is most deceptive, treasure is most desired,
> gold for each of men, and the old man is wisest,
> the one who has experienced much, wise with the
>   passing years.
> Misery is amazingly clinging, the clouds fleeting.

In this catalogue, we have the assertion that 'the powers of Christ are great' and that God sends the crops at harvest-time. Early critics saw the *Maxims* as a semi-pagan text in which Christ is subordinated to Fate, an argument which can be made simply by removing the full stop after 'the powers of Christ are great'. But surely the point is that these superlatively powerful and impressive elements of weather and chance are subject to the disposition of God who is involved in the created order but not subject to it. What is significant here is that God and Christ are not part of the catalogue of superlative things, but outside that particular theme. So the Creator is not spoken of in the same way as the creation.

WHAT IS TRUTH?

By a seamless transition the poem turns from the natural world of the seasons and weather to the world of humankind, where after a couple of lines the superlatives peter out. But here we have one of the more perplexing lines: truth is most deceptive. The next lines are banal enough: treasure is most valuable, the old person wisest because they have experienced most in life. Is the poet drawing a distinction between truth and wisdom? Is this a kind of medieval postmodernism which sees only the 'will to power' in the use of words like 'truth'? Scholars have tried to get round this problem by changing the Old English word *swicolost*, 'most deceptive', to *switolost*, 'most obvious'. But this avoids an issue which recurs in wisdom literature.

When for example the proverb 'honesty is the best policy' was coined, it was deeply ambiguous. On the one hand, it meant what it seems to mean: being honest is the best way of conducting human relationships. But in Shakespeare's language 'policy' meant trickery, deceit; and 'politician' meant a schemer. So Shakespeare's 'scurvy politician' was not a member of the government with a skin problem, but an out-and-out shyster, a shameless trickster. As a result, 'honesty is the best policy' also meant 'you'll fool more people by telling the truth than you will by telling lies' or 'honesty is the best way of tricking people', with the underlying idea that people expect others to tell lies, so telling the truth is a double bluff. This ambiguity about honesty and truth demands that we think closely about what truth is. That is the purpose of the saying in the poem, and it is one of those lines that hits the reader between the eyes.

EVERYTHING IN ITS PLACE

The poet then moves on to another catalogue which links items with their location in the scheme of things.

> Courage belongs in a warrior, the sword endures
> battle with the helmet. The hawk belongs on
>   the glove,
> the wild creature stays there. The wolf belongs in
>   the forest,
> a wretched solitary creature; the boar belongs in
>   the wood,
> a creature strong of tusk; the good man earns
>   reputation
> in his own land; the javelin belongs in the hand,
> the gold-decorated spear; the jewel gleams on the
>   ring,
> big and prominent; the stream mingles with
>   the waves
> in the sea; the mast belongs on the ship,
> the sail-yard hangs heavy; the sword belongs on
>   the lap,
> a splendid piece of ironwork; the dragon belongs in
>   a burial mound,
> old and proud of its treasures; the fish belongs in
>   the water,
> producing its spawn; the king belongs in the hall,
> sharing out rings; the bear belongs on the heath,
> old and terrible; the river flows in a grey flood
> downhill; the army stands together,

a band of men focused on glory; faithfulness
   belongs in the warrior,
wisdom in a man; the wood blossoms with fruit
in the land; the hill stands green
upon the earth; God belongs in the heavens,
the Judge of deeds; the door belongs on the hall,
the wide mouth of the edifice; the boss belongs on
   the shield,
strong protection for the fingers; the bird plays
up in the sky; the salmon glides
in the pool with the trout; the shower from
   the heavens,
mixed with wind, comes down into the world;
the thief moves about in darkness; the monster
   lives in the fens,
alone in the land. A woman, a girl seeks out her
   lover with secret art
if she does not wish to prosper among her people
so that she is obtained with rings [that is, married].
   The salt sea surges,
flows with mighty tides around each and
   every land,
the cloud and the sea. Cattle breed and propagate
on earth; the star shines bright
in the heavens, as God commanded it.

There are some possible connections between the items in
this list. For example in the last two, cattle on earth and the
star in the heavens, there is a contrast in the place – earth
and heaven – where the God-ordained activity takes place. A
similar contrast could also be operating between the cattle on
earth, and the sea and the sky of the previous verses. Contrast
is more obviously used in the lines which follow these, as we

shall see. But it is principally the catalogue itself which imposes structure on the phenomena. Things are defined by what they are and what they do: this allows the infinite variety of things to be encompassed and tamed. The catalogue is a way of getting your head around the ideas and minimizes the fearfulness, the anxiety of the unknown and chaotic. Plainly if we can predict the habitual location of the dragon, we can avoid accidentally tripping over one and annoying it.

The catalogue also imposes a way of interpreting phenomena. The poet does not distinguish between epistemological (things to do with belief) and empirical (things to do with observation) categories, for example. Things that are empirically obvious, like the wolf belongs in the forest, the boar belongs in the wood, the mast belongs on the ship, the door belongs on the hall and so on, are put together with things that we would certainly classify differently: courage belongs in the warrior, loyalty belongs in the warrior, wisdom belongs in a man, and God belongs in the heavens. We might dispute altogether the idea that dragons belong in burial mounds. The poet puts together the empirical, the ethical, the religious and the folkloristic. He might have done this in some sense accidentally, believing these things to be as self-evident as the others; or he might have done it deliberately, to suggest that these things *should be* as self-evident as the others, that it *should be* as natural for a man to be brave and loyal and wise as it is for fish to live in water. The possibility of either of these intentions cannot be ruled out. But it is clear that the structure of the catalogue raises questions about interpretation.

CONVENTIONAL WISDOM

This catalogue is characterized by the verb phrase *sceal on*, 'belongs in/on', or *sceal*, which I have translated as a present

tense indicating habit or custom, as in 'endures', 'mingles' and
so on in the lines above. This verb occurs in practically every
line of the section of text. Just as this structure starts to break
down, the poet inserts the lines on the behaviour of the
young noblewoman who defies convention. It may be no accident that she keeps company with the thief and the monster
before, as she is robbing her family of the dowry of rings, and
will end up alone. Her case is also followed by the surging of
the sea, a metaphor for sexual passion even today, and the
mating of beasts. It is possible to press the conjunction of
these images too far, but one of the main functions of wisdom
literature is to challenge us to see the connections between
things.

A brief catalogue of contraries follows this:

> Good is against evil, youth is against age,
> life is against death, light against darkness,
> an army against an army, enemies against
>   each other,
> people who hate each other dispute over land,
> inflicting injury. The wise man thinks
> about the conflicts in this world; the
>   criminal hangs
> properly to repay the crime he had committed
> against humanity.

Again we see the contrasts of the brief proverbs we looked at
earlier. But the theme has taken a darker turn: antagonism
seems to be built into the structure of life, and strife is the
normal outcome. At the end, although the wise man thinks
about these important things, human knowledge gives
out, and God alone knows the mysteries of death and the
hereafter.

KNOWN AND UNKNOWN

The last section of the poem turns to final things. One of the features of these lines is the very effective way they bring the poem to an end. This could be a problem for poets who were composing for listeners rather than readers, especially when there was no narrative or storyline to reach an ending. The Anglo-Saxon poets tended to turn to death and the life here-after, a pattern of ending found in a dozen or more poems. But as well as ending with the end of life, the wisdom poem ends with the end of human knowledge. The Creator alone knows about these things, the Lord alone knows, and no one else can say for sure.

> The Creator alone knows
> where the soul will go afterwards,
> and all the spirits who go before God
> after the day of death to await judgement
> in the embrace of the Father. The future is
> hidden and secret; the Lord alone knows these
>   things,
> the saving Father; no one comes back
> here under the roofs who can say for sure
> to people what might be the Lord's decree,
> the establishment of the victorious where he
>   himself dwells.

There is an echo here of one of Job's laments: Job says,

> As a cloud vanishes and is gone, so he who goes
>   down to the grave does not return.
> He will never come to his house again; his place
>   will know him no more.

Despite echoes of Christian doctrine and biblical ideas, though, the Christian content of this part of the poem is slightly odd. We can illustrate this by comparing the eschatological doctrine of *Beowulf* with this passage in the *Maxims*. The relevant passage of *Beowulf* comes at the end of the introduction to the poem before the action involving the hero begins. Plagued by the monster Grendel, the Danes try everything, even making sacrifices to idols, to solve the problem. The Christian poet remarks that this was a terrible thing to do, but not their fault because they did not know the true God. Then he uses two maxims to generalize the situation and close this episode:

> Such was their habit,
> the hope of the heathen. They thought of hell
> in their hearts. They did not know the Lord,
> the Judge of deeds, they were not acquainted with
>   the Lord God,
> and did not know how to worship him, the
>   Guardian of the heavens
> and Lord of glory. Woe it is for the one who must
> through persistent enmity thrust his soul
> into the embrace of the fire, expect no change
> or alteration of any sort. Well it is for the one who
>   is permitted
> after the day of death to approach the Lord
> and to ask for protection in the embrace of the
>   Father.

There are quite a few of these *Wa–Wel* ('woe–well') maxims in Old English poetry and prose. They are predominantly eschatological, that is to say, they are concerned with death, judgement, heaven and hell. They frequently occur in pairs which contrast eschatological destinies. The point about this passage is that the picture derives almost entirely from the Bible, particularly the gospels. There is a grim play on the word *fæthm*, 'bosom, embrace', for example, which contrasts the embrace of the Father with the embrace of the fire in the *Beowulf* passage. The embrace of the Father enjoyed by the souls of the blessed is an extension of the intimacy enjoyed by Christ himself, 'who is in the bosom of the Father', John 1:17 – this is the only reference to the embrace of the Father in the New Testament. The embrace of the fire can be found in Matthew 25:41 and elsewhere, where the fire is eternal, hence the hopelessness and changelessness of those who suffer it. The stark contrast between the two states is characteristic of the New Testament.

Now compare this with *Maxims II*. It uses more theological jargon: souls and spirits, judgement, saving, truth, the ordinance of God and so on. It also uses the notion of the embrace of the Father. But the idea of hell is notably missing; this poem concentrates only on the nice bits and gives a long shrug about the rest, declaring that nobody knows, nobody comes back to tell us about it, and nobody can be sure what it is going to be like. Now it obviously suited the *Maxims* poet to end on a note of definite ignorance. He has been asserting throughout the poem the patterns of things that can be known, things that are observable, and he wished to counterbalance that by the expression of humility before the invisible and unknowable.

Appropriate though some humility is in the context, the poet's humility would be a little too agnostic for most of the Anglo-Saxon homilists, for example. For them, St Paul's maxim 'we walk by faith and not by sight' (2 Corinthians 5:7) would be conclusive. In putting forward gospel doctrine about the hereafter, the poet of *Beowulf* was walking by faith. The

Maxims poet was rather hedging his bets, choosing what he wanted to believe, or perhaps choosing to express what most people generally believed. He was walking by sight, and what he could not see, he took the liberty of remaining undecided about.

WISDOM AND LIFE

It has become evident in this chapter that there were different kinds of wisdom in Anglo-Saxon England: the popular and the learned. There were certainly many points of contact between them, and much borrowing. Both were valued, but when they came into conflict, Anglo-Saxon and later scholars preferred to assert the authority of Bible and Church. We have seen how in one case Wulfstan specifically argued against the proverbs he had heard among the people. Nevertheless, by arguing against them, Wulfstan also preserved the proverbs. And although we can see significant differences between the popular and the more directly biblical treatment of the theme of eschatology in *Beowulf* and the *Maxims*, both poems came to be recorded. We all make decisions on what core beliefs we live by, and those core beliefs come from a variety of sources: tradition, faith, science, experience. The Anglo-Saxons were not so dogmatic that they could not value wisdom from divergent sources. Contemporary faith-communities, from those who believe only in science to those who believe only in religion, might benefit from a reorientation towards wisdom.

A discourse on wisdom

Each virtue has its special graces, and the graces
and dignity that it has, it very readily grants to
each of those that love it. In this way, wisdom is
the highest virtue and it has within it four other
virtues: firstly, caution; secondly, moderation;
thirdly, courage; fourthly, justice. Wisdom makes
those who love it wise and cautious and moderate
and patient and just, and it fills the one who loves
it with every good quality. Those who have power
in this world cannot do that; they cannot out of
their wealth grant any virtue to those who love
them, if they do not have it in their nature.

This passage is taken from King Alfred's Old English translation of Boethius's *Consolation of Philosophy*, and it is spoken,
appropriately, by Wisdom. The virtue of wisdom is very evidently a practical thing here. Wisdom gives those who love it
certain mental qualities, to be sure, but those qualities only
become known in action.

5

MONKS

MONKS AND LITERATURE

The overwhelming majority of Old English literature is known now because monks wrote it down. This has some drawbacks. For example, we have to assume that there was a lot of interesting material that never came to be written down, perhaps because it was thought unsuitable by the Church. And a good deal more was written down, but was lost or destroyed in the attacks on the monasteries from the Vikings down to the Dissolution under Henry VIII. But though there is a strong bias towards obviously religious books (sermons, service books, Bibles, religious poetry, saints' lives) in what survives, there is nevertheless a large quantity of material which is not specifically religious, and some of it is translated in this book. The point here is that apart from a few secular scribes employed by kings and nobles for writing legal documents and accounts, monks were the people who wrote and copied literature. What we now have, we have because monks preserved it for us. That in itself implies that some monasteries at least were open and curious about the world, prepared to see the value of things not immediately concerned with the religious life, not narrowly focused only on the tiny world within the walls of the monastery. This is worth remembering as we look at that tiny world in this chapter.

MONASTICISM AND CONVERSION

Monasticism was at the heart of Anglo-Saxon Christianity. The conversion of the Anglo-Saxons was largely accomplished by the preaching of monastic missions. St Augustine of Canterbury and the missionaries from Rome were monks, and when he tells us about them, Bede makes it clear that the monastic life they lived was derived from the communal living of the earliest Church in the Bible:

> As soon as they had established themselves in the house given them [by King Æthelberht], they began to emulate the life of the apostles and the early Church. They spent their time in constant prayers, vigils and fasting, preaching the word of life to everyone they could. They despised all goods of this world as unnecessary, and accepted only vital necessities from those they taught. They practised everything they taught in their lives, and were prepared patiently to suffer and even to die for the truth that they preached.

When the Anglo-Saxons became Christians, the monastery became an attractive alternative to secular Christianity, especially for the nobility. According to the occasional references we get to such things in the sources, Bede's monasteries of Wearmouth and Jarrow had around 600 monks at the height of their fame, and others had yet more.

MONASTIC VISION AND PROVISION

What was it that made the monastic life so attractive? This is a difficult question to answer simply. The motives of those who took it up differed widely. But once Christianity had taken hold, its teachings gave new and important meanings to familiar ideas. Bede wrote the history of the abbots of his own monastery, the joint foundation of St Peter at Monkwearmouth and St Paul at Jarrow. The founding father of the monastery was Benedict Biscop. Bede's picture of Benedict is one which points up the contrasts and parallels between the secular and the spiritual life:

> He was born of noble stock among the English, but was of no less nobility of mind, and was raised up to merit keeping the company of angels forever. Briefly, when he was a thane of King Oswiu and received from him possession of a gift of land in accordance with his rank at about the age of 25, he despised the passing possession in order that he might gain the eternal; he looked down on earthly military service with its perishable reward in order that he might serve as a warrior for the true King and deserve to have a lasting kingdom in the heavenly city; he left home and family and land for the sake of Christ and for the sake of the gospel in order that he might receive a hundredfold and have eternal life; he rejected the service of the flesh in marriage in order that he might be able to follow the pure Lamb in the glory of virginity in the kingdom of heaven; he refused to beget mortal children by bodily means, being predestined by Christ to bring them up by spiritual teaching, heavenly sons in eternal life.

As Bede writes it, the odds are rather heavily stacked in favour of the religious life. Every one of the rewards promised by Bede and the Bible passages he quotes are eternal as against the temporary satisfactions of the world. But Benedict knew what he was giving up: power and wealth, lordship and loyalty in the warband, home and family, bodily pleasures and domestic joys. He had served his time in the army, and had earned his land; now he felt it was time to join the ranks of the heavenly hosts and use his land for the establishment of the monastery. He did it with his eyes open, as one who could see and compare the rewards of earth and heaven. Such vision was compelling.

Benedict was immensely influential in determining the kind of monasteries that were established in Northumbria. He visited Rome and scoured the Continent for books that would ennoble and enrich his monasteries and provide the spiritual food that they needed. So the Northumbrian monasteries became places of learning, and the list of books to which Bede had access at Monkwearmouth shows it to have had one of the finest libraries of the early Middle Ages. Benedict also gave them relics of the saints and apostles, vestments and vessels; and, less tangible but equally valuable, access to the Pope and his influence with the Northumbrian kings.

More than that, Benedict imported masons from France to build churches of stone, and also glaziers to make windows. As Bede remarks, the glazier 'was a kind of craftsman unknown in Britain up to that time'; and the Anglo-Saxons were not in the habit of building in stone even if they had masons. So the monastic buildings would have had novelty value, as well as being by far the most impressive buildings the Anglo-Saxons had ever seen. They represented visually the values that monasticism held to: stability, regularity, enduring and vital community.

And indeed this representation was taken further by
Benedict, who made a point of bringing sacred pictures from
the Continent,

> so that all people who entered the church, even if
> they were illiterate, wherever they looked, would
> be able to contemplate the friendly faces of Christ
> and his saints, though only in a picture. Or would
> be able to call to mind a more lively sense of grati-
> tude for the Lord's incarnation. Or, with the
> crucial moment of the Last Judgement as it were
> before their eyes, would remember to judge them-
> selves more earnestly.

The monastery was a little outpost of heaven, where those who
wanted to could see 'as in a mirror, darkly' the glory to come.

FORMATION OF CHARACTER

But all this is not perhaps as significant as the people who
lived in the monasteries and especially those who were
abbots. Bede is most affectionate in his portrait of Ceolfrid,
the abbot who shaped his early life. But Ceolfrid's co-abbot
at the monastery's other site at Wearmouth, Eosterwine, is
described briefly, showing his delightful character:

> Eosterwine took over the care of the monastery of
> Wearmouth in the ninth year from its foundation.
> He remained there for four years until his death.
>   He was a nobleman, but he did not, as some do,
> allow the privilege of nobility to give rise to boast-
> ing and despising others; but rather, as befits a
> servant of God, made it serve his desire for greater

nobility of soul ... Though he had once been a thane of King Ecgfrith, he laid aside the concerns of the world, laid down his weapons and took up spiritual warfare, and remained so humble and so like all the other brethren that he was pleased to winnow and thresh with them, to milk the cows and sheep, to be gladly and obediently employed in all the work of the monastery in the bakery, the garden or the kitchen. When, moreover, he was promoted to the role of abbot, he still kept the same attitude to everybody that he had before, according to the warning of the wise man who said, 'Have they made thee ruler? Be not lifted up: be among them as one of them, gentle, courteous and kind to all.'

He certainly corrected those who sinned with the discipline of the Rule when he had to, but he would rather earnestly warn them with his habitual kindness, so that they had no wish to sin and cloud the brightness of his countenance with their disturbances. Often as he went about the business of caring for the monastery, if he came upon the brothers working he would immediately join with them in the work: either taking the plough-handle to guide the furrow, or beating iron with the hammer, or shaking the winnowing-fan, or helping in some other way.

He was a strong and healthy young man, with a gentle way of speaking. He was moreover cheerful of disposition and generous, with a pleasant appearance. He ate the same food as the other monks, always dining in the same building; he slept in the same place in the common dormitory as he had before he became abbot. And even when he was struck down with illness, and was aware, from clear signs, of his coming death, he still lay for two days in the dormitory of the brethren.

Only for the last five days until the time of his death did he put himself into a more secluded place. Then coming out on a certain day and sitting in the open, he summoned all the brethren to him, and with his usual tender-heartedness, he gave them the kiss of peace, while they wept and mourned for the loss of so good a father and shepherd. He died on the night of the 7th of March, when the brethren were busy singing the early psalms of praise. He was 24 years old when he entered the monastery, and lived there 12 years: for seven he fulfilled the duties of a priest, and for four he had the rule of the monastery. And thus, leaving 'his earthly body and mortal limbs' he entered the kingdom of heaven.

This passage tells us almost as much about life in the monastery as it does about Eosterwine. In the early days, it was the monks who farmed the land and did the various labouring tasks that were necessary. A range of domestic and agricultural jobs is mentioned here, as well as the customary worship. More alarmingly, the humility of monks like Eosterwine, expressed in a refusal to take more comfortable and secluded quarters when suffering illness, made the spread of infectious disease almost inevitable. Indeed Bede later describes a disastrous plague which all but wiped out the entire foundation. Eosterwine died at the age of 36, an average lifespan for a man of the times.

The description given by Bede might seem conventional. Like many other monks, Eosterwine is a nobleman who has set aside his earthly military service for the sake of spiritual warfare. Like many others who became abbots, he is humble, sharing fully in the common life of the brethren. He also knows that his death is approaching, as the saints so often do. But there are several things on which Bede is silent: he says nothing about Eosterwine's learning. This is a conventional thing to mention, as is asceticism and extreme self-denial, as are spiritual disciplines. But Bede does not mention any of these. What we have here is in many ways unconventional in the terms of the literature of the time, but something we can recognize: a real person. This healthy, gentle, kindly, active, busy, loving, sociable man is someone we would like to know, and would enjoy being with.

Bede, then, is telling us about someone affectionately remembered for the quality of his life. Bede was very committed to learning: he delighted in books, and loved his learned abbot, Ceolfrid. He tells us that Ceolfrid doubled the size of the library that Benedict Biscop had endowed the monastery with, adding books which included three whole versions of the Bible, and selling another book to King Aldfrith for eight hides of land (somewhere between 500 and 1,000 acres) for the monastery, such was the quality of its workmanship. The detail of these transactions and acquisitions shows Bede's interest. The lack of this sort of detail might be thought to detract from Eosterwine's character. But in his learned and erudite way, Bede pays his respects to Eosterwine, quoting from Virgil's great epic poem, *Æneid*, book VI, when he says, 'leaving "his earthly body and mortal limbs" he entered the kingdom of heaven'. The quotation is from a discussion in the underworld between the father Anchises and the son Æneas. Anchises tells Æneas of the divine and fiery nature of the life of man and beast, provided it is not hampered by 'earthly bodies and mortal limbs', which drag it down. So

Bede recognizes the spiritual quality of Eosterwine: active in body, but not hampered by bodily concerns, whose spirit flies back to its source as he dies.

LATER MONASTICISM

Early monasticism in Anglo-Saxon England was rather different from the monasticism which was revived under King Edgar in the second half of the 10th century after the Viking attacks had all but snuffed out the institution. The great monasteries of the north-east of Bede's day, with their traditions of learning and asceticism, were wiped out. So was something less easily definable – a sense of enthusiasm, being part of a movement destined to conquer the earth, idealism perhaps. At any rate, when King Alfred tried to re-establish monasteries in his reign towards the end of the ninth century, he could not raise enough Englishmen to occupy one and had to import men from abroad. It was only when a spell of peace followed the first period of Viking activity that enthusiasm for monasticism returned.

Part of the problem was that Christianity had become secularized. It was clear that the Vikings had to be resisted by all possible means, and that meant it was the Christian duty of some people to fight, some to farm and some to pray. All of these duties were Christian callings, and if any one of them gave way, disaster would result. Consequently, the clear divide between the secular and spiritual callings became blurred at the edges. And in the absence of monasticism, Christianity had to be maintained by other means. It is difficult to trace the precise developments, but it is evident that people clung to their faith, they met together for worship, they taught their children and kept Christian traditions.

When monasticism was revived in the times of King Edgar the Peaceable, 959–75, with the help of three saintly bishops, Dunstan, Æthelwold and Oswald, it reacted rather strongly against the secularism which had ensured the survival of Christianity. Towards the end of Edgar's reign, an agreement was drawn up by a committee under the chairmanship of Æthelwold, which set out new regulations for monasteries. This, the *Regularis Concordia* or 'Monastic Agreement', is a new version of the Benedictine *Rule* for monks, with additions reflecting developments since the *Rule* was composed. The main development was that the monasteries had now become de-secularized to the extent that their entire business was worship.

The Monastic Agreement is pre-eminently concerned with the liturgical duties of the monks, with very little of Benedict of Nursia's original focus. The everyday work on the land that occupied Eosterwine and Benedict himself has gone from the monastic life, and has been allocated to servants. Monks are now responsible for worship, and prayer for the king. Monastic life is much more institutionalized than it ever was before. Monasteries, as landowners holding royal charters, are now far more part of the fabric of society. They are almost solely responsible for the schooling of youths, and indeed, one of the sections in the prologue to the Monastic Agreement anticipates modern child protection policies in trying to ensure the proper treatment of the boys in the monastic schools.

For the rest of this chapter, we will observe the implications of these changes in monastic life in two documents: one a charter which tells a gripping story of struggle and intrigue between monasteries and involving the king; and the other a dialogue for teaching the boys of the monastery school their Latin.

MONASTIC RIGHTS

Anglo-Saxon charter-writers are not noted for their narrative skills. They usually employ a few legal phrases and state very baldly and concisely what the purpose of the charter is, often the transfer of land ownership. A little colour is added in the maledictions at the end on anyone who tries to go against the provisions of the charter. But this charter from the time of Harold Harefoot (before 1040, probably 1038) is quite extraordinary in telling a story full of vivid detail.

This charter makes publicly known that King Harold took [the port of] Sandwich from the possession of the monastery of Christchurch, Canterbury, into his own hands. He kept it for himself about twelve months — two full herring seasons, at least — completely against God's will and that of all the saints who rest in Christchurch. And he suffered sadly for it afterwards.

At this time Ælfstan was abbot of St Augustine's Canterbury. With his gold and silver, and by means of cunning, he secretly arranged with Steorra the king's steward that the third penny of the toll at Sandwich should go to him, Ælfstan. Archbishop Eadsige, when he found out about this, together with the community of Christchurch, decided that the monk Ælfgar from Christchurch should be sent to King Harold. The king was very sick at Oxford, and was not expecting to live long. Lyfing, Bishop of Devon, and Thancred the monk were with him. The messenger from Christchurch came to Bishop Lyfing, and he, with Ælfgar, Oswerd of Harrietsham and Thancred, went to the king straight away. They said that the king was very guilty before Christ in ever having taken anything from Christchurch which his predecessors had granted to it. They mentioned the case of Sandwich, which had been taken into the king's possession. Hearing this message, the king grew dark with anger as he lay, and afterwards swore by Almighty God and all the saints that it was never his will or by his action that Sandwich should ever have been taken from Christchurch. Then the truth was clear: the plan was not the king's but that of other men. Indeed, Abbot Ælfstan had advised the men who wanted to deprive Christchurch.

Then King Harold sent the monk Ælfgar back to Archbishop Eadsige and to all the monks of Christchurch. The king greeted them all in God's name and his own, and commanded that they should possess Sandwich as completely and immediately as they had ever had it in any other king's day – rents, water-taxes, shore-taxes, fines, and all the rights, to the fullest extent that any king before had held them.

When Abbot Ælfstan heard of this, he went to Archbishop Eadsige and asked for his mediation with the community of Christchurch in the matter of the third penny. So they both went to the brothers and asked the community that Abbot Ælfstan might be allowed the value of the third penny of the tolls in return for a gift of 10 pounds. But they all unanimously opposed the suggestion that this should be done, despite the fact that Archbishop Eadsige was more on the side of Abbot Ælfstan than Christchurch. When he saw that he was not getting anywhere, Ælfstan asked to be allowed to build a wharf opposite Mildred Field as a defence against the fury of the tides. But the whole community completely and immediately rejected the idea, and Archbishop Eadsige left the decision to them.

So then Abbot Ælfstan came with a huge army of workers and had a great trench dug at Ebbsfleet, in the hope of having a navigable channel for ships flowing there, as the community had at Sandwich. But it did not work for them in the least, because the one who labours against the will of Christ, labours in vain. So the abbot left it at that, and the community kept what was theirs. This is all true, in the sight of God, and St Mary and all the saints who rest in Christchurch and St Augustine's; believe it who will. Abbot Ælfstan never sought in any other way to get the third penny from Sandwich.

May God's blessing be with us all for ever. Amen.

All kinds of intrigue are going on in this episode, and it is in many ways a rather unedifying spectacle. The tolls from Sandwich were a major source of necessary income for the monastery of Christchurch. They supported the monks in their duty of worship. It appears that the older (and more prestigious) monastery of St Augustine's wanted to 'share' the profits to the extent of taking a third, and in order to do that bribed the king's steward and deceived the king. When the king was disabused as to the entitlement of Christchurch to the dues of Sandwich, and he reinstated their rights, Abbot Ælfstan still tried to con them. He tried to persuade them, with the archbishop on his side, and to buy them off; he tried to syphon off their dues by asking for permission to build a wharf of his own, and when that failed he tried to make an alternative channel by force.

The Christchurch monks knew what was right, despite the fact that the archbishop and the king, as well as the abbot of St Augustine's, seemed to be against them. God acted in accordance with the law, and Abbot Ælfstan found it to be true, that 'unless the Lord builds the house, its builders labour in vain' (Psalm 127:1). The conviction of the Christchurch monks that God is on the side of the powerless, and has vindicated his people in this situation, stands out. King, archbishop and Abbot Ælfstan all merit some criticism, but this charter is a remarkably objective and confident document in which the story speaks for itself.

Clearly the monastic life in the 11th century had become politicized. Monasteries needed land and income to maintain themselves, and some rather underhand business went on in this case in the attempt to ensure the wealth and prestige of the institutions. The old monasteries, self-contained and as independent of the world as they could be, have gone. For all their rejection of secular work, the new monasteries have taken a role more central to the secular world of Anglo-Saxon England, and they are dependent on that world for their well-being.

LIFE INSIDE

For a glimpse of life inside the monastery, we turn now to Ælfric's *Colloquy*. Ælfric was an abbot in one of the new monasteries, and a profoundly learned man. The substance of the *Colloquy*, as we have seen in chapter 2, is a discussion of the occupations of the men employed by the monastery and more widely. The boys in the school pretend to be the characters – oxherd, shepherd, merchant, huntsman and so on, whom we have already met – to practise their Latin vocabulary. But the *Colloquy* is introduced and concluded by comments and questions directed at the boys as themselves, that is, as boys in the monastic school. This is how the *Colloquy* starts:

> We children pray you, O teacher, that you teach us to speak proper Latin, because we are ignorant and we speak ungrammatically.
>
> *What do you wish to speak?*
> What do we care what we speak, as long as it is proper and useful speaking, not pointless or bad.
>
> *Do you wish to be whipped in the process of learning?*
> It is better for us to be whipped for the sake of learning than not to know things at all. But we know you are kind and do not intend to inflict beatings on us unless you are compelled to.
>
> *I ask you, and what will you say: what work do you have?*
> I am a professed monk, and seven times each day I sing the hours with the brethren, and I am occupied in reading and singing; but among all this I nevertheless want to learn to speak in the Latin language.

No doubt there is an element of wishful thinking on the part of Ælfric here. What teacher would not want to have children begging to be taught, and happy to be beaten so long as they could learn their Latin? But we learn several things from this passage. Even in monastic schools, and until relatively recently, corporal punishment was considered to be an essential pedagogical method. The topic returns at the end of the *Colloquy*.

Another thing is evident: the boys could take a full part in the liturgy of monastic life without understanding what they were singing. A mid-11th century service book in Corpus Christi College, Cambridge, known as 'The Red Book of Darley', has Latin texts with most of the headings and instructions in Old English, which suggests that the boys were not alone in being able to recite Latin without understanding it. One of the strategies that has been employed over many centuries is for someone to write a 'crib' in between the lines of the original, and that has been done in the manuscript of the *Colloquy*; ironically, the 'crib' is now used to teach English students Old English. Another thing we learn is that the cycle of monastic services, derived from Psalm 119:164, 'seven times a day I praise you', is unchanged, though as we see later, the services take longer than they used to.

After the discussion of the occupations, the focus returns to the boys:

> *Well, children, how does this speech please you?*
> It pleases us very well. But you speak in a very profound way, and what you say is over our heads: so speak to us according to our understanding, so that we can understand the things you say.

> *I ask you all, why are you so eager to learn?*
> Because we do not want to be as stupid as the beasts that know nothing but grass and water.

And what do you want?
We want to be wise.

In what sort of wisdom? Do you want to be sly or shifty in deceit, cunning in speaking, artful, wily, speaking well but thinking evil, habitually using smooth words but nurturing guile inside, like a tomb with painted monuments on it that inside is full of stench?
We do not want to be wise like that, because he is not wise who fools himself with his own deception.

So how do you want to be wise?
We want to be kind without hypocrisy and wise so that we turn away from evil and do good things. Moreover, you examine us more searchingly than we are able to take at our age. So speak to us according to our custom, not this deeply.

I will do just as you ask. You, boy, what did you do today?
I did many things. In the night I got up from my bed when I heard the bell and sang nocturns with the brethren. After that we sang the lauds of the day and of all the saints. After these we sang prime and the seven psalms with litanies and chapter-mass. Then we did terce and the mass of the day. After these we sang sext, had our food and drink and sleep, and then we got up again and sang nones. And now we are here before you, eager to hear what you will say to us.

When do you intend to sing vespers or compline?
When it is time.

Were you whipped today?
No, I was not, because I kept alert.

And your companions?
Why do you ask me that? I dare not reveal our secrets to you. Each one knows whether he was whipped or not.

What do you eat in the day?
I am still allowed to eat meat, living under the rod.

What else?
Vegetables and eggs, fish and cheese, butter and beans, and all clean things I eat with great thanksgiving.

You must be very greedy if you eat everything put in front of you.
I am not so much of a glutton that I am able to eat every kind of food in a single meal. Sometimes I eat this food, sometimes that, but in moderation as befits a monk, not with greed for I am not a glutton.

And what do you drink?
Ale if it is available, but water if not.

You do not drink wine?
I am not that rich that I can buy wine for myself. Besides, wine is not a drink for the young and foolish, but for the old and wise.

Where do you sleep?
In the dormitory with the brethren.

Who wakes you up for nocturns?
Sometimes I hear the bell ringing and I get up.

Sometimes the master arouses me roughly with the rod.

Well, children and delightful scholars, your master urges you to be obedient to the divine teachings and to behave yourselves in seemly fashion everywhere. When you hear the church bells, go obediently; go into church and bow humbly to the holy altars; stand properly and sing together; pray for your sins; and go out into the cloisters or to your classes without horseplay.

This passage roves over the concerns of the monk: the services, diet and drink, order and propriety, and in a patchwork of scripture references, the pursuit of wisdom. The services evidently take up most of the monk's waking hours. Since they start in what we would think of as the middle of the night, the problem of sleepiness is one that recurs in most of the monastic rules: the Monastic Agreement makes provision for an official to patrol the premises, noting things not put away or individuals not properly awake. Not implausibly for boys, the *Colloquy* pays attention to food and drink: as youths, the boys are allowed meat, which is denied to older monks, and there is a variety of other food in moderation. And the boys are taught to make a distinction between craftiness of speech and eloquence, and urged to behave in seemly fashion.

The *Colloquy* better represents the daily realities of monastic life than the motivation behind it. The affectionate tone of the *Colloquy* is partly concealed by the formality of the teacher-pupil exchange. The focus on the daily round of worship tends to distract attention from Christ, whom the monks spent their lives worshipping. And the sense that this life is safe and ordered and purposive only comes through in the negative aspects of beatings and routine.

PRIVILEGE

But the monastic life was a privilege in Anglo-Saxon England. It was a life that demanded everything of a person. It could be hard and unpleasant, yet it bred saints and scholars who found its discipline an aid in their desire to live a life of obedient worship. It produced scholars like Bede, men of simple devotion like Eosterwine, teachers like Ælfric. It was not a perfect system by any means, but it preserved and encouraged the growth of a living faith. Discipline is not something the modern world cherishes much outside sport. But it is a means of spiritual growth.

The General Introduction to the Benedictine Office in Old English

Divine service is established in the Church's ministries according to the canonical pattern, as a duty for all people in holy orders. At all times God should be praised, and in every place they should earnestly cry out to God. But nevertheless there are specific hours established for the special purpose that if someone is too busy to do it more often, at least he should fulfil this daily duty. Just as David said, *Seven times a day I will praise you.* That is, 'Seven times a day I sang praise and honour to you, Lord.' It will be too seldom, if it is ever less frequent than seven times a day that we praise God: that is, once first at dawn, then again at terce, and at midday, and at nones, and at vespers, and at compline and at matins. It is not within the capacity of any person to be able to praise God more than he deserves. Yet it is necessary for all of us that we earnestly serve him and wait upon him as far as we are able and know how to.

The Benedictine Office takes the seven canonical hours for worship as its framework, based on Psalm 119:164. Seven signifies completeness in the thought-world of the Bible. But the Old English writer goes on to suggest that seven times of worship is the bare minimum for a day. Much more than this is appropriate, for, as he says, it is not possible to overdo praise of God. Thus the apparently repetitive daily round of worship becomes at once complete and incomplete. Complete in that it is an acceptable minimum, but incomplete in that it can never be adequate to the sublime task it sets itself. It is enough, the writer concludes, if we all do our best.

6

BEDE

BEDE'S LIFE

We know virtually nothing about Bede that he does not tell us himself or reveal through his works. We have to guess from his words when he was born, and it seems to have been 672 or 673; he died at a good old age for the time, 62, in the year 735. This is what he tells us about himself at the end of what most people regard as his greatest work, his *Ecclesiastical History*:

I was born on the land of this monastery [of St Peter and St Paul, Monkwearmouth and Jarrow], and when I was seven years old I was given into the care of the most reverend Abbot Benedict, and then of Ceolfrid, by my kinsfolk, to be educated. Since that time I have passed my entire life in this monastery, giving myself wholly to the study of the scripture. In the course of observance of the discipline of the monastic Rule, and the daily singing of the services in the church, it has always been a pleasure to me to learn or teach or write. I was made deacon at the age of 19, at 30 I was ordained

priest, both times through the ministry of the most
reverend Bishop John at the direction of Abbot
Ceolfrid. From the time I was ordained priest until
I was 59, I have taken care, for my own benefit and
that of my brothers, to compile brief extracts from
the works of the venerable Fathers on the holy
scriptures, and to add notes for clarification on
their sense and meaning.

A pretty dull life, then. But this account masks by its simplicity things tragic, heroic and saintly. Bede never makes reference to his natural parents, speaking only of Abbot Ceolfrid
as a father. It is probable that Bede came to the monastery as
an orphan, and it was there that he found the love and care,
the brothers and the father that children need.

An anonymous *Life* of Abbot Ceolfrid gives us another
insight into Bede's early life. It tells of a plague that occurred in
686, when Bede was about 13; this plague wiped out all the
monks in the monastery except Ceolfrid himself and a boy.
Both loved to sing the services and antiphons, but in these des-
perate circumstances, Ceolfrid suspended the antiphons; this
sad state of affairs went on until Ceolfrid could not stand it any
longer, and they sang, each taking a part, until new monks
joined the monastery. That boy must have been Bede, since
he tells us he kept his monastic vow of stability, never moving
away from the monastery where he made his profession.

In due course, in the monastery over which
Ceolfrid ruled, all who could read, or preach, or say
the antiphons or responses were carried off, with
the exception of the abbot himself and one little
boy. This boy had been trained and taught by the
abbot, and is now at present in priest's orders at the

same monastery, where he properly commends the
abbot's praiseworthy deeds to all who wish to
know, by his writing and discourse. The abbot,
made terribly sad by the aforementioned plague,
ordered that the original rite should be suspended,
and that they should complete all the psalms without the antiphons except at vespers and matins.
When this had been done for the space of a week
with many tears and complaints on his part,
he could endure it no longer, and decided to re-
establish the psalm-singing with antiphons according to custom. And what he had decided he put
into effect with much exertion and difficulty for
all, on the part of the aforementioned boy and
himself, until he was able to train himself, or
gather from elsewhere, sufficient brothers to carry
out the *opus dei*.

When Bede himself came to write his *Lives of the Abbots* of
his monastery, he made his affection for Ceolfrid evident.
Ceolfrid bequeathed to Bede a love of the liturgy and the
psalms particularly. The monastic life was centred on worship;
the *opus dei*, 'God's work', or the regular round of worship, was
the purpose of the monastery. In this, the singing of the
psalms was especially important. It might be imagined that
singing the entire psalter almost every week for an entire lifetime could diminish the fervour with which the psalms were
sung. Not so for Bede. A story about him told by Alcuin in a
letter possibly to the monks at St Peter's, Monkwearmouth,
Bede's own monastery, shows how eager he was to sing the
psalms:

It is said that our teacher and your patron, the
blessed Bede, said, 'I know that the angels visit the
canonical hours and the meetings of the brothers.
What if they should not find me there among the
brothers? Will they not say, "Where is Bede? Why
does he not come to the appointed devotions with
his brothers?"'

That sense of the presence of the angels, which doubtless
encouraged Ceolfrid and Bede to persevere with the singing
when there were just the two of them, stayed with Bede all his
life.

BEDE'S DEATH

Bede was held up as a model for the monastic life after his
death. But during his lifetime, he was revered as a teacher,
respected as a scholar, and widely suspected of being a saint.
All these things are evident in a letter about the death of
Bede, written by a pupil of his called Cuthbert to a friend of
his, Cuthwine. Cuthbert became abbot of the monastery later
in life, but it is uncertain who Cuthwine was. This is the substance of Cuthbert's letter:

He gave us, who were his students, daily lessons,
and spent the rest of the day in singing the psalms
as far as possible. He cheerfully devoted the whole
of the night to prayers and giving thanks to God,
except when a little sleep interrupted him. And
when he woke up, he would immediately mull over
again the familiar strains of the scriptures, without
fail reaching out his hands to God in thanksgiving.

I confess that I have never seen with my eyes or heard with my ears anyone so faithful in giving thanks to the living God. He was indeed a blessed man! He used to chant the proverb of St Paul the apostle saying, 'It is a dreadful thing to fall into the hands of the living God', and many other things from holy scripture, by which he urged us to wake from the sleep of the soul by thinking beforehand of our last hour. He spoke of the terrible departure of the soul from the body in our language, for he was familiar with our songs:

Before that inevitable journey no one becomes wiser in his thoughts than is necessary for him, in order to ponder, before his departure
what, after his death-day, may be the judgement on his soul, whether good or evil.

He used to sing antiphons for our comfort and his own...

When the Tuesday before Ascension Day came, his difficulty breathing became much more severe, and a slight swelling in his feet appeared. He nevertheless taught us all that day and dictated cheerfully. And he said among other things, 'Learn quickly, "for I know not how long I shall continue, and whether after a while my Maker may take me away".' But it appeared to us that he knew well when his end would be.

Thus he spent the night watching in thanksgiving, and when dawn broke, on the Wednesday that is, he commanded us to continue earnestly the writing we had started. It took us until nine

o'clock, and at nine o'clock we walked in procession with the relics of the saints, as the custom of
the day required. One of us was with him and said
to him, 'There is one chapter of the book you were
dictating left, but it seems to me that it will be difficult for you if I ask any more of you.' But he said,
'It is easy. Take up your pen and sharpen it, then
write quickly.' And he did so. At three o'clock in
the afternoon he said to me: 'I have a few precious
things in my box: some pepper, napkins and
incense. So run quickly and bring to me the priests
of our monastery and I will distribute these little
things that God has given me.' I did so with trepi-
dation. And when they were there, he spoke individually to them, urging them and pleading with
them to pray and offer masses for him regularly.
And they freely promised to do so. But they were
all mournful, and every one wept...

He spent his last day joyfully until the evening.
Then the aforementioned boy, called Wilberht,
said once again, 'Dear master, there is one sentence
remaining unwritten.' And he said, 'Write it.'
After a while the boy said, 'I have just written it.'
And he said, 'Good. It is finished – you have
spoken the truth. Take my head in your hands, for
it is a great pleasure to me to sit over against my
holy place, where I used to pray, so that I can call
upon my Father as I sit there.' And so, on the floor
of his cell, singing 'Glory to the Father and to the
Son, and to the Holy Ghost' and so on, he
breathed his last. And indeed we may believe
without question that as he always worked here for
the praise of God, so his soul was carried by the

angels to the joys of heaven for which he yearned. All who saw or heard of the death of the blessed Bede, our father, said that they had never seen anyone reach the end of his days in such great devotion and peace, since, as I heard it myself, for as long as his spirit was in his body, he chanted 'Glory to the Father' and other songs to the glory of God, and constantly reached out his hands to God in thanksgiving.

You should know, too, that much more could be said or written about him, but now my unlearned tongue makes for short speeches. In due course, though, I intend with God's help to write more fully about him that which I saw with my own eyes and heard with my own ears.

This letter explores quite beautifully some of the tensions of the Christian view of life and death. Bede's life was complete. He has spent his last days doing what he has always done: teaching, dictating, praising and thanking God, singing the psalms, encouraging his pupils. He knows he is about to die, and when the last sentence of Wilberht's book is complete, he quotes the dying words of Jesus from the cross: 'It is finished.' And yet, as with all the saints, there is much more to be said about him. Cuthbert promises something like a saint's life in his last paragraph, and indeed there was a cult of Bede in later Anglo-Saxon times, and several churches were dedicated to him. But perhaps this letter expresses the essence of his life, its completeness and fullness, more than an embellished saint's life ever could.

The letter records for us the one piece of Old English verse that Bede might have composed himself. *Bede's Death Song*, as it is known, is recorded in more manuscripts than any other

Anglo-Saxon poem. It teaches directly the need for everyone to be prepared for death. Judgement is certain, whether good or bad. With it Bede also quotes from the Epistle to the Hebrews 10:32, then thought to have been written by St Paul, about how terrible death can be. Yet he shows in his own death the serene confidence of one who has thought on, pondered and prepared for death. Bede, the fatherless, goes to be with his Father. Leaving the little 'holy place' of his monastic cell, where he loved to be, he goes to the larger joys of heaven, in peace and praise.

Bede's death, in its devotion and completeness, is a model of monastic integrity: a fully rounded life. This is perhaps why the letter, while full of affection, lacks the raw edge of grief. Centuries later Thomas Ken tried to teach the boys of his school the same lessons as Bede's life and Cuthbert's letter:

> Teach me to live that I may dread
> The grave as little as my bed:
> Teach me to die, that so I may
> Rise glorious at the awful day.

SCHOLARSHIP

Bede was the greatest scholar of his day, and the list and variety of his books is daunting: he wrote on Latin grammar and metre, the sacred sites of the Holy Land, lives of saints, particularly his hero St Cuthbert, a history of the abbots of his own monastery, the great *Ecclesiastical History*, a treatise on the tides and astronomy, major works on chronology and calculation of times, and all this in addition to his extensive list of biblical commentaries, sermons and studies of theological questions. Bede was the scholar who popularized the BC/AD dating system, where before people had counted the years of the kings. Without him we probably would not be thinking of a third millennium. Bede's sermons were used in monastic liturgies all over Europe for centuries, and St Boniface, the great Anglo-Saxon missionary to Germany, pleads with his correspondents for them to send any book they can find by Bede to him, to help in his work.

> Now we exhort you with eager desire to comfort our sorrow, as you have done before, by sending us some spark from that light of the Church which the Holy Spirit has kindled in your land: namely, that you will be so kind as to send us some portion of the treatises which Bede, that inspired priest and student of the Sacred Scriptures, has put forth in his writings. Most especially, if possible, his lectionary for the year [the homilies], which could form a convenient and useful manual for us in our preaching, and the Proverbs of Solomon. We hear that he has written commentaries on this book.

HIGH REGARD

Why, we might ask, was Bede so highly regarded as a scholar and as a Christian writer? One reason is that, unusually for the medieval period, he was scrupulous about using and acknowledging sources. He assembled and read the Fathers of the Church in his biblical scholarship. He wrote to churchmen all over England for information, he sent a monk to the papal archives in Rome to gather details of the correspondence between Pope Gregory and St Augustine of Canterbury relating to the conversion of England. He gives the names of the people from whom he heard the stories he included in the

Life of St Cuthbert or the *Ecclesiastical History*. He puts notes in the margins of his work with source references. In some ways the footnote traditions of modern scholarship can be traced back to Bede, and for him it meant immense labour, but it was the labour of a man utterly committed to the honest and joyful pursuit of knowledge in the service of God and God's people.

CLARITY

A second reason for the high regard in which Bede is held is contained in his outline of his life. 'From the time I was ordained priest until I was 59, I have taken care, for my own benefit and that of my brothers, to compile brief extracts from the works of the venerable Fathers on the holy scriptures, and to add notes for clarification on their sense and meaning.' He was strongly aware of the tradition he was working in, he looked not for recognition but for usefulness; not for flourishes of style, but for clarity. In his preface to his exposition of the book of Revelation, he says this:

> Thinking to consult the slothfulness of our race of the Angles, which not so long ago in the days of the blessed Pope Gregory received the seed of the Faith and cultivated it, so far as reading went, lukewarmly enough, I have determined not only to elucidate meanings, but express statements tersely, since plain brevity rather than prolix disputation is wont to stick in its memory.

I have given this passage in the translation of Claude Jenkins, because it captures the flow of Bede's writing. The image in the first part of the sentence comes from Jesus's various parables about sowing seeds, with the seed of faith lazily cultivated by the Anglo-Saxons. The image brings together everyday life, because most people were involved in agricultural pursuits, and Christian truth. Then it goes on to respond: bearing in mind this laziness in reading, Bede will explain things clearly and briefly. And despite the appearance of this sentence in translation, it is, for the Latin writers of the time, both clear and brief.

His sermons, so anxiously sought by Boniface, are not dramatically original, but they are precisely what he claims: 'brief extracts', carefully assembled, discussed and presented for the edification of the hearer or reader. A better and more complete summary of basic Christian doctrine would be hard to find. This is what Boniface needs for his missionary work, because Bede covers everything of importance. He does not always do it in the way that modern readers would either expect or necessarily find helpful. In the prologue to his commentary on the books of Samuel, he starts at the very beginning with the statement that Elkanah, the father of Samuel, had two wives, and by way of explaining his approach he says:

> Now if we bring forth only the old things from the treasury of the scriptures, that is, if we take heed only of the literal forms and figures after the manner of Jewish people, how shall we find there rebuke for our daily sins, or consolation among the increasing troubles of this world, or spiritual doctrines among the innumerable uncertainties of this life? For we discover through reading or hearing only the clear words of the book of the blessed Samuel, that one man, Elkanah, had two wives. For us especially, whose life has been established by the church to be celibate and to remain absolutely

set apart from the embrace of a wife, how shall we
find rebuke, teaching and consolation, if we do not
know how to carve out from these words and ones
like them the allegorical meaning by which our
inner life is restored?

Bede proceeds to allegorize the two wives, one as Israel, the
other as the Church, rather as St Paul allegorizes Hagar and
Sarah in the Epistle to the Galatians, 4:21ff. He is working
within a tradition, but essentially he is making a connection
between holy scripture and holy lives. He believes that scripture is important and has a purpose in the life of individuals
and of a society.

LEARNING AND HOLINESS

A third reason for Bede's high standing is that he learned first
to practise, before he ever started preaching. He recognized in
St Cuthbert, as we shall see, that gift of integrity of life which
he longed for himself. Cuthbert, and Bede following him,
practised the truth, before – and while – preaching it. In his
commentary on the book of James, 1:19, 'Everyone should be
quick to listen, slow to speak and slow to become angry', Bede
wrote,

From here on, James instructs the listeners by
moral precepts. And quite properly he starts by
urging everyone to be more ready to lend an ear to
someone who is teaching than to open their mouth
to teach. For it is foolish for anyone to wish to
preach to others what he has not learned himself.
He who loves wisdom should first ask for it from
God, as James has urged earlier. Then as a humble

hearer he should look for a teacher of the truth.
And in the meantime he should restrain his tongue
most carefully not only from idle speech, but even
from preaching what he has only recently learned
of the truth.

Bede took this to heart, learned the lesson he taught, because
as he says, he did not start his writing on the biblical books
until after he was ordained priest, long after he had composed
important works on other subjects. He saw his biblical and
theological work as the most important of his life: something
he had to earn the right to do.

Bede was immensely learned. But he had a healthy awareness of the limitations of scholarship. He was perfectly aware
that brilliance of mind was of less value than holiness of life.
Though he wrote beautifully, with imagination, and with a
razor-sharp intellect, he seldom left the Holy Spirit out of
consideration. In his commentary on Luke, he writes,

Unless the Lord enlightens the hearts of the hearers, the teacher labours in darkness. If the weapons
of debate do not serve the word of heavenly grace,
the preacher throws the javelin of his voice in
vain. For the faith of people is not quickened by
the wisdom of the perfectly formed sermon, but by
the gift of God's speaking through it.

Bede recognized many of his teachers and friends as great
scholars, but he never referred to the first abbot of his
monastery as 'learned'. This is not damning with faint praise.
Benedict Biscop travelled all over Europe to provide the
monastery with the means of scholarship, scouring the
Continent for books and relics, as Bede tells us. It is evident

throughout his writings that he loved and revered the man. Bede valued scholarship, but he valued holiness more.

This sense of the limitations of learning is part of his theology, which focuses on eternal life and truth. Bede's book *On the Tabernacle* explores the allegorical and mystical significance of the Tent of Meeting, in which the Israelites worshipped God during their wanderings in the desert. A passage based on Exodus 26:35, 'Place the table outside the curtain on the north side of the tabernacle and put the lampstand opposite it on the south side', says this:

> The table and the lampstand designate the temporal benefits of God, with which we are refreshed and illumined in the present time, that the grace of our merits might increase as a result of being strengthened and sustained by these things for a while, so that we may be enabled to come to eat the bread of angels in heaven and to see the true Light of the world. Both of these are outside the curtain, for only in this life do we have need of the Holy Scriptures, or teachers, or the other sacraments of our redemption, but in the world to come, where the Lord will tell us plainly of the Father (that is, he will show us the Father openly), and where as John says, *we shall see him as he is*, there will be no need of the external props of salvation, because God Almighty, dwelling internally in his elect, will shine upon them as the Light of life, satisfy them as the Bread of life, and raise them up to perpetual blessedness, leading them into the joy of his kingdom.

The table is the place where food is put, and the lampstand gives light to the proceedings. The table represents the

Eucharist, where bread and wine refresh the Christian. The lampstand represents the enlightenment of the mind given by the teaching from the Bible. But the table and the lampstand in Exodus are placed outside the curtain of the tabernacle. Inside the curtain is the Holy of Holies, the very presence of God. Plainly, then, the food and light which the table and the lampstand represent are for this life. But when the Christian enters God's presence, God himself becomes the Bread of life and the Light of life: the 'external props' will be unnecessary in the presence of Reality.

Bede took his own theology to heart, as we can see from Cuthbert's letter. But there is something deeply moving about this exposition. It is beautifully simple in the development of its ideas, and clear and economical in its expression. It opens Bede's mind before the reader, as Bede sees the curious and often tedious physical details of the tabernacle in the Bible point towards spiritual truths. Jesus says in John 5:39, 'These are the Scriptures that testify about me', and clearly Bede agrees. As his exposition progresses, and the biblical furniture gives way to the means of grace in this life, and the sacraments and teachings of this life give place to the great Presence behind the curtain, Bede moves from mere words to the goal of all his endeavour. And Bede recognizes that in the presence of Christ, the delight which he expresses in learning and teaching and writing in his autobiography will be overwhelmed by greater joys. His scholarship, passionate and profound, is only for the here and now.

IMAGINATION

A fourth reason for Bede's repute is that he writes not only with skill and clarity and moral strength and conviction, but especially with imagination. When he writes stories, they are plausible and vivid. The story of the conversion of Northumbria is one of his best. King Edwin has called a council to decide what ought to be the religion of the land, and the heathen chief priest, Coifi, says this:

'O king, consider this matter which is now being preached to us. I tell you truly that, as far as I can learn, the religion which we have hitherto professed has neither power nor profit in it. None of your people has devoted himself more diligently to the worship of our gods than I have, and yet there are many who receive greater benefits and greater honour from you than I do and are more prosperous in all the things they do. If the gods had any power they would have favoured me more, as I have always made it my business to serve them with greater zeal. Therefore it remains to be said that if on examination these new things which have now been preached to us are better and more effectual, we should accept them without any delay.'

Another of the king's chief men agreed with this argument and with these wise words and then added, 'It appears to me, O king, that the present life of man on earth, in comparison with that time which is unknown to us, is like this. You are sitting at the feast with your noblemen and warriors in wintertime. A good fire is burning on the hearth in the middle of the hall and all inside is warm, while outside the winter storms of rain and snow are raging. A sparrow flies swiftly through the hall. It comes in at one door and quickly flies out through the other. For the time it is inside, the storm and wintry tempest cannot touch it, but after the briefest moment of quiet, it vanishes from your sight. It flies out of the winter storm and quickly into it again. So this human life appears for a short time: of what is to follow, and what went before, we are completely ignorant. So if this new doctrine gives us more certain information, it seems right that we should follow it.' Other elders and counsellors of the king said the same things by divine prompting.

Coifi added that he wished to listen still more carefully to what Paulinus himself preached about God, and when Paulinus had done that at the king's command, Coifi exclaimed, 'I have long since realized that there is nothing in our religion. For the more earnestly I sought the truth in our cult, the less I found it. Now I publicly confess that in this preaching the truth clearly shines out which can confer on us the gifts of life, salvation, and eternal happiness. Therefore I advise your majesty that we should instantly abandon and burn down the temples and the altars we have consecrated to no advantage.' Why need I say more? The king publicly allowed Paulinus to preach the gospel, and renouncing idolatry, professed faith in Christ.

We know that Bede was particularly interested in the conversion of the English. This is the central topic of his *Ecclesiastical History*, from which this passage comes. It is most likely that someone sent Bede the basic information about Edwin's council. He would have known some of the traditions about who was there and how it all turned out. What he has done in this story is to present two entirely different arguments for Christianity and how it might have appealed to the Anglo-Saxons. Through Coifi, he presents the pragmatic argument that heathenism does not work and is intellectually inconsistent. Coifi is a hard-headed, hard-nosed, business-like character, who wants hard evidence. The other speaker represents a more poetic side to the Anglo-Saxon character. He shows the yearning for emotional and intellectual security in a hostile world through the delicate image of the sparrow.

Bede's art gives us a believable picture of how the Anglo-Saxons responded to the gospel. There are hundreds of stories like this in Bede's *Ecclesiastical History*, and the remarkable thing is that, for all the imagination he has put into the writing, these stories remain the backbone of historical investigation today.

BEDE AND TIME

Bede spent his life preoccupied in many ways with time. His *Ecclesiastical History* not only deals with the past of the English, but puts history into a framework which has an ending, a goal, in the kingdom of God. His biblical commentaries, as we have seen, move from the incidentals of the text and its historical situation towards a universal and eternal meaning. In his works on the calculation of times and the calendar, there is a focus on the dating of Easter, the point at which time and eternity come together. On this last matter, Bede wrote at length and occasionally with uncharacteristic intemperance, letting his passion for, and pride in, scholarly accuracy and orthodoxy get the better of him. But if, as he saw it, human history, past, present and future, turns on Christ's death and resurrection at Easter, then to celebrate it at the wrong time was to upset the balance of the world.

For Bede, though, time always gives way to eternity. At the end of his very substantial book *The Reckoning of Time*, he writes:

> And so our little book concerning the fleeting and wave-tossed course of time comes to a fitting end in eternal stability and stable eternity. And should those who read it deem it worthy, I ask that they commend me in their prayers to the Lord, and that they behave with pious zeal towards God and their neighbour, to the best of their ability, so that after temporal exertions in heavenly deeds, we may all deserve to receive the palm of heavenly reward.

And so, for himself, he prays at the end of the *Ecclesiastical History*,

> I pray you, good Jesus, that since you have graciously given me your words of knowledge sweetly to drink, so also you will grant in friendship that I might finally come to you, the fount of all wisdom, and remain forever in your presence.

FOCUS

Bede was committed to education and scholarship, and did his best to further both. He wrote effectively by keeping in mind the people for whom he was writing. For scholars he wrote sharp, incisive, well-documented arguments. For ordinary people he wrote colourful, clear and imaginative works that are as far from stuffy, churchy writing as it is possible to get. He knew the value of holiness, and the role of discipline in achieving it. He lived for 55 years in one place, and seven times every day, except when illness intervened, he would attend divine worship. His life was a focused life. He was well aware that such focus was a privilege that not everyone could enjoy, and so he tried to make connections between ordinary life and the teachings and sacraments of the Church.

From an early age, he seems to have cultivated the virtues he sets before us in his writings. His honesty, orthodoxy and simplicity derive from a basic attitude of humility. Bede knew there were limits to his knowledge. And he understood that the gospel is for everyone, and is not best served by complexity and showing off. Humility is not incompatible with great achievement, but the humble person values achievement less than the gift of God. So it was for Bede. And perhaps above all other things, Bede looked steadfastly towards the goal of his life, doing all he could to prepare himself and others to be and live forever in the presence of God.

An Old English version of the Gloria

Glory.
May glory and praise, thanks and love,
power and mercy, and all heartfelt affection,
the peace of the righteous, be attributed to you far
   and wide
throughout all peoples, and may your own praise
be made splendid in the world; for you are able to
   rule
all earthly powers and those of the sky,
the wind and clouds. You righteously rule
   everything.
Be to the Father and to the Son and to the Holy Spirit
You are the Father of mercies and the Guardian of
   the spirit,
the Guide of life, the Ruler of light,
utterly apart from sin; so also your glorious Son
by pure generation, the King over all,
is confidently blessed, with the Teacher of
   learning,
the high Comforter of the heart, the Holy Spirit.
As it was in the beginning
As at the beginning, the Lord of humankind,
pure and powerful, was the beauty and joy
of the whole world. You made that known,
when you, eternal God, alone created
the heavens and the earth by your holy power,
the lands and the sky above and all things.
You put on the earth very many kinds of creatures
and divided them into a multitude;
eternal God, you made all created things

in six days, and on the seventh you rested;
then was your beautiful work accomplished
and you yourself consecrated Sunday
and you celebrated it as a help to many.
All those who know Christian customs
and that highest command, keep and observe
with holy devotion the high and holy day:
the day is honoured in the Lord's name.
Is now and ever shall be
And now and forever your true works
and your great power make evident to many –
as your widespread skills, they declare this
over all the world: God's handiwork
will remain forever, and will grow as you
    command.
All holy instruments and Christian books,
the entire earth, all praise you
with pure voice; and we humans proclaim
here on earth, 'Praise and thanks to God,
eternal love, and the glory due to you!'
World without end
And for ever and ever the king
lives and reigns in glory. And these remain
    forever:
his chosen ones, the great splendours of the Holy
    Spirit,
bright angels and glorious gifts,
true peace, the thanksgiving of spirits,
kindness of heart; there is the perfection of love.
The heavens by your eternal word
are everywhere full of holiness,
and likewise the works of power that you yourself
    made
are visible and evident throughout the earth.
Amen.
We all say this truly:

You are properly king by pure origin,
pure and powerful. You, mighty God,
revealed your nature when you created man,
and put into him breath and spirit,
gave him language and intelligence and various
    kinds of fruits;
  you demonstrated your abilities. Such is the power
    of Christ.

Bede occupied himself with singing the *Gloria* as he was dying. This poet has richly elaborated the Latin phrases with all kinds of doctrinal and practical applications. Bede would have appreciated this, and especially the reference to 'Christian books', which he read and wrote with such devotion and skill.

7

SAINTS

The traditional stories of early saints, along with the Bible, the liturgy, monasticism and the learning of the Fathers of the Church, came to Anglo-Saxon England with the Christian missionaries from Rome and Ireland. They were part of the Christian tradition, and the Anglo-Saxons welcomed the whole tradition. The Anglo-Saxons delighted to commemorate their ancestors and their glorious deeds in battle. When monasticism took root, with its vow of celibacy, this characteristic respect for the past of one's family naturally sought some expression. And in some senses, the saints provided the spiritual ancestry for which the Anglo-Saxons longed, just as the monastic community provided the 'family' which the monk had otherwise to do without.

The Anglo-Saxon church understood perfectly well that every Christian is chosen by God and made holy, a 'saint' in the general sense. We have already seen the impact that holiness of life and character had on people when they encountered it. But both the early and medieval Church recognized that some were particularly marked by the grace of God in their lives, and that these people were spiritually powerful. These were the 'saints' in the particular sense. The

Anglo-Saxon liturgy rapidly became populated not only with the ancient saints and martyrs of early Christianity, but also with the saints, and in due course martyrs, of British and Anglo-Saxon Christianity. And 'populated' is not a mis-chosen word: these saints 'live and reign' with Christ, but have particular interests on earth, as we shall see. Anglo-Saxon England became dotted with holy places dedicated to the memory of the saints; but these were also places where the saint's powers were revealed.

THE SAINT'S LIFE

The written life of a saint is an important document. Generally people of particular holiness become known and respected in their lifetime. Certainly this was the case in Anglo-Saxon England. During their lifetime, they also do things that people remember. Something they do or say has a marked impact, and the people they have helped treasure the memory. After the death of the saint or holy person, the sto-ries are told and often become more remarkable in the telling. Other people in need turn to the saint and find that praying at his or her tomb, or touching some physical possession of the saint, or some item that has touched the holy body, has miraculous effect. Some people in distress have dreams in which the saint comes to their aid.

All this would be recorded in the life of the saint, and the document itself bore witness to the reverence in which the saint was held. The life was the first step towards making pop-ular devotion to the saint official, the first recognition by the Church authorities that the revered person was a holy saint of Christ. In later times, a written life became part of the labori-ous and technical process of canonization, and though the process was much less formal in Anglo-Saxon times, this nevertheless was what was going on. Another part of the process was the 'translation' or moving of the body to a place of greater honour, or somewhere where it could be more accessible. Often the body was found to be untouched by decay when it was moved.

The life was important as part of a process. One of the many reasons for the greatness of St Cuthbert in Anglo-Saxon times was that he had one life written about him by a monk of Lindisfarne and two by Bede (one in verse and another in prose), and the story of his miracles was continued in much later times by his community and various historians. This points to another important fact about saints: although the life is a significant factor in ratifying the cult, the saints have never finished doing the kind of things they did in their lifetime. The very name, the life of the saint, neatly expresses this. The saint, having died, is not dead, but alive in heaven and continuing the work he or she did before. So no life can be definitive. There is always more that can be said.

The lives of the saints collect the stories that circulated about them, the miracles they and their relics performed. To be frank, such stories often inspire more scepticism than faith in contemporary readers. Some things we find odd, all the visions, and apparitions of demons, and trips to hell. Other things we find slightly repugnant, like the attention paid to bits of the saint's body: St Edmund's severed head, or St Oswald's severed hand, the water the saint's body was washed in, or pieces of their clothing. Along with all this goes an insistence on the miraculous: nothing is too simple or too complex to be explained as a miracle.

ENCHANTMENT

But to understand this kind of literature and to see its enchantment, it helps to be aware of the conditions in which it flourished. The stories are most often the cherished memories of people whose lives have been touched. Stories improve in the telling, and a good story has a strong and simple plot. More than that, stories reinforce a world view: they fit and adapt events into a pattern that people can recognize; so that even if the hearers have not personally experienced attacks of demons, they know that demons are deceitful, and when exposed, they are cowardly and smell horrible. Moreover, the stories meet needs. Anglo-Saxon medicine was not very sophisticated, and cures for many simple diseases were unknown: stories of the saints curing people by touch, or from a distance by their word, give people hope in a dangerous world.

If we can read the saints' lives with these things in the back of our minds, that will help us enjoy them more. But before we piece together some stories from the lives, one more thing should be noticed. This is that the life is literary genre. Like the novel, or the sonnet, or the play, it has certain conventions. As a child the saint is set apart or marked out as someone special; in youth, the saints are challenged to make the prophecies about them come true by entering the religious life. They live lives of self-denial and their holiness and good deeds make an impact on those around them. No saint willingly takes on the responsibility of being a bishop or abbess or abbot, because they are humbly aware of their inadequacy. They have visions or the gift of prophecy or healing. They die a holy death, and miracles happen when their help is called for, or their relics are touched. Sometimes they appear to people in times of need, and give advice which helps them. Most of these conventions derive ultimately from the Bible – the miracles, for example, are often modelled on or explained by reference to similar events in the Bible – but some do not. It is customary for the writer to say in the preface that although he is ill-equipped for the task, he has been all but forced to write the life, and he begs the reader to excuse the infelicity of his style.

The conventionality of the saints' lives makes some things stand out. Stories that are unconventional can be included; a convention can be given a twist or denied altogether; the number or range of a certain kind of story can tell us something about the individual saint in a way that the ordinary stories cannot. So we can enjoy the saints' stories in the way that people enjoy the set characters and locations, along with the amazing twists of plot, in soap opera. But in addition we can appreciate that there are real people behind most of the stories in saints' lives – people trying to make sense of their feelings and of the world, people trying to find hope and purpose in a harsh and difficult environment.

CONVENTIONS

There can hardly be a better example of the convention of the self-deprecatory preface to the saint's life than the one by Eddius Stephanus, writing the *Life of Bishop Wilfrid*. Wilfrid was a contemporary of Cuthbert, a powerful speaker and missionary, self-consciously important, and a noble bishop. Cuthbert was quite the opposite of Wilfrid in temperament, preferring solitude and asceticism to any kind of show. But though the two were so different, Stephanus copied more or less word for word the preface of the Lindisfarne monk's *Life of St Cuthbert*. Having named the bishop and abbot who asked for the *Life of Bishop Wilfrid*, he goes on, in the words of his predecessor:

If only the result was as good as I wanted it to be!
This work is demanding and my abilities in understanding and eloquence are small. But although
the service may be below the standard your command should require, it at least pays the debt of
obedience I owe you.

The only words added to the original in this passage are 'and
eloquence', and although Eddius is not a writer of Bede's class,
he is nevertheless competent in this department. So he naturally denies what he could perfectly reasonably claim.

One of the things that makes Bede so attractive as a writer
is that he does not go for this conventional false modesty. He
knew the convention perfectly well. But he was also very well
aware that although he was writing his prose *Life of St
Cuthbert* at the request of the community of Lindisfarne, they
had chosen him to write it as the best writer available. So he
took a rather unconventional tack:

I have not written anything about so important a
man without the most determined examination of
the facts. Nor have I presumed to send anything to
be copied for general reading without the closest
scrutiny of reliable witnesses ... I have tried to put
down on parchment what I found out to be reliable
truth in clear and simple words free of all ambigui-
ties and strained effects. And I took care to bring
what was written before your community [at
Lindisfarne] so that whatever was false could be
corrected by the authority of your criticism, and
whatever is true might be approved.

Most writers of saints' lives make some claim to be telling only the truth. But Bede goes far beyond that: he has investigated the stories, put them together in straightforward language, and submitted them for approval. He claims the *Life* to be more of a joint effort than most. But his own contribution has been important in two particular areas, research and writing, and with perfect justice he does not want to make light of these things.

BIRTH AND CHILDHOOD

Some portent usually accompanies the birth of the saint, or something in their childhood reveals that their future will be saintly. An apparition of fire burned over the house when Wilfrid was being born, much to the alarm of the local men. Breguswith, the mother of St Hild of Whitby, the royal abbess of a justly famous monastery, had a dream in which she lost everything, including her husband who was to die in exile. But Hild's mother found in her dream a jewel under her clothes. The jewel shone so brightly that the whole of Britain was made light. And so Hild's future role in holiness and in teaching and bringing the light of the true faith to all England, and, through the famous Whitby council, to the Celtic lands, too, was foretold.

St Nicholas is now known as Santa Claus. Nicholas was born into a wealthy patrician Roman family and flourished during the reign of Constantine, the first Christian Roman emperor in the fourth century. His life shows his liking for young people, and his ability to appear in different places to help people. Santa developed from St Nicholas, and obviously retains these two traits. The Old English *Life of St Nicholas* tells how at a very early age he showed his future holiness and modelled piety for children:

As soon as the child Nicholas was born and was suckling at his mother's breast, it became his custom each Wednesday and Friday only to feed once during the day, and to leave the rest for the day after. By this divine miracle, indeed, was revealed how glorious a man he was to become. Then he grew up and began to flourish. And as he grew from childhood to maturity he paid no attention to this world's riches. He spent some time with his father and mother, and sometimes he went on his own to church. And whatever he heard read from the holy scripture in church, he lodged it all in his heart, and it remained fixed in his memory.

We are not told what his mother might have felt about his uncomfortable habit, but St Nicholas is one of the few who practised fasting while still a baby!

Another saint, Guthlac (674–714), was descended from East Anglian royalty. After an exemplary childhood and early monastic training he became a hermit at Crowland, where he lived in a burial mound, fighting the devil. He suffered many temptations from the devil himself and evil apparitions of various kinds, but by the simple eloquence of the words of scripture and faith he put them all to flight. His childhood was marked by goodness and restraint of speech:

During the time of his early childhood, he tried to talk as children do. But he was never any trouble to his parents or nurses, or to the groups of children of his own age. He did not copy the insolence of the children, the chattering nonsense of the mothers, the empty stories of the ordinary folk, the foolish bellowing of the country people, the worthless deceits of flatterers, or the various calls of birds as children of that age usually do. But empowered by extraordinary wisdom, he had a happy face, a pure mind, a kind heart and a sincere appearance. He was affectionate to his parents, obedient to those older than himself, loving to his foster-brothers and sisters. He led no one astray, blamed no one, made no one stumble, repaid no one evil for evil. He was habitually even-tempered.

The writer of Guthlac's *Life*, Felix, seems to have shared little of Guthlac's sweetness of disposition. He has used his eloquence to show the foolishness of ordinary people, yet his hero plainly had that kindliness which encourages everyone. But though Felix has on this occasion given way to sarcasm about others, it is entirely possible that on reading his own work, he was rebuked by Guthlac's example.

MONASTIC LIFE

After being called to holiness in childhood, the saint usually enters the monastic life and shows great commitment to the spiritual life, and usually greater self-denial than others. One of the remarkable things about St Æthelthryth was that she entered the life of asceticism before she became a nun and abbess. Bede tells her story briefly:

King Ecgfrith married a wife called Æthelthryth, daughter of King Anna of the East Saxons, whom we have often mentioned. Anna was a deeply religious man, noble in thought and deed. Æthelthryth had been wife to another man before this, a prince of the South Gyrwe called Tondberht. But a short time after they were married, he died, and Æthelthryth was given to King Ecgfrith. She lived as his consort for 12 years, but nevertheless preserved intact the glory of perfect virginity. This was confirmed to me when I asked, because people doubted that it was true, by Bishop Wilfrid of blessed memory. He told me that he had absolute proof of her virginity, because Ecgfrith had promised to give him much money and land if he could persuade the queen to consummate the marriage, for he knew that she loved Wilfrid more than anyone. There is no need for us to doubt that this happened in our own time, when we learn from reliable accounts that it sometimes happened in past times with the help of the same Lord who has promised to remain with us 'even to the end of the age'. And by the sign of the divine miracle, in which her flesh did not decay in the grave, it is evident that she remained untainted by fleshly contact with any man.

Bede shows no sympathy whatever for Ecgfrith, who had good reason to feel cheated by Æthelthryth's decision. The saint's life privileges self-denial in the quest of holiness above all other things, and Bede lived the celibate monastic life himself, so perhaps he was blind to the problems Æthelthryth caused the king.

Bede's reference to past examples of virginity may be to the virgin martyrs, of whom St Juliana was one, and whose story is told later in chapter 9 of this book. Bede also makes neatly explicit the link between purity in life and the incorruption of the body after death, one of the most common miracles attributed to the saints. But he also sees that both things need some substantiation. The evidence of Bishop Wilfrid that Ecgfrith pleaded with him, to no effect, rings true. Certainly Wilfrid's biographer, Eddius, makes Wilfrid's refusal to use his influence with the queen one of the main reasons for the estrangement of king and bishop, and for the king's decline in power.

MIRACLES

Miracles were the stock-in-trade of hagiographers, the writers of saints' lives. Gregory the Great, who sent the Christian mission under St Augustine to England in 596, was widely revered in the country that in part owed its faith to him. He was a great pope, a practical theologian, and had the insight of a true pastor. In one of his renowned books, the *Dialogues*, he tells of, and discusses, the life and miracles of St Benedict who was the writer of the monastic *Rule*, and founder of many monasteries. But Gregory had a somewhat reserved attitude to miracles closer to home, which showed itself when Augustine wrote to him from England for guidance on the subject. He writes,

> I know that almighty God, for love of you, has worked great marvels for the people that he wished to call his elect. It is necessary that you should have both fearful joy and joyful fear over this heavenly gift. Rejoice that the souls of the English are attracted by the outward wonders to inward grace. Fear that in the process of working these signs, the unsteady soul may elevate itself presumptuously, and that which raises it to outward honour may be the cause of its fall into vainglory ... Whatever powers of working signs you have received, or will

receive, they are not given to you, but through you
for the salvation of others.

The earliest life of St Gregory was written by a monk of
Whitby, at the end of the seventh century. One of the problems he faced was the relative lack of miracle stories about
Gregory, which raised questions as to whether he should be
considered a saint, and indeed whether the story of his life
would not be found inadequate without them.

> With the help of God, we will consider in what
> way our holy teacher St Gregory, a man incompa-
> rable, should be venerated by us as a saint. Desiring
> to write a book on that question, though we have
> heard of few miracles in the account of his deeds,
> we pray that our readers will not be disgusted if we
> praise such a man rather fulsomely. For there are
> many who are in the habit of bringing into consid-
> eration the miracles of the lives of the saints, and
> who judge their holiness and merits by their signs.
> And this is not unreasonable: for God, who is 'glo-
> rious in his saints', often makes those whom he
> loves more than other people shine more than
> other people by the miracles they perform.

In the following chapter, the writer goes into a long and
rather convoluted argument as to why Gregory should be
honoured. But in this passage above, he makes it clear that
people expected miracles in saints' lives, and would feel short-
changed when they did not get them. And our writer has
rather more scruples than most about inventing stories. He
nevertheless is able to scrape a few together, so that Gregory
is properly honoured.

Eddius Stephanus, Wilfrid's friend and hagiographer, writes at length about Wilfrid's exiles and political struggles with successive kings and archbishops. But he still finds time to record miracles of Wilfrid. On one occasion he restored to life a child whose mother pleaded with Wilfrid to baptize him. On another, a young man who was involved in the building of Wilfrid's church at Hexham, fell and was restored to life.

When the masons were building the highest walls of the house of God, a young man from among the servants of God slipped from a pinnacle of incredible height, fell to the earth, and landed on the stone floor, the life crushed out of him. His arms and legs were broken, all his limbs disjointed, and he lay drawing his last breath. The masons, according to the instructions of the holy bishop, who was moved to tearful prayer, quickly carried him outside on a stretcher, thinking he was dead. And immediately at a signal, the whole of the bishop's following gathered together, and the bishop, standing among the brothers, said, 'Let us all together, full of faith, ask God that he might return the soul of this boy to his body, so that he might live, just as he granted it to St Paul.' So they prayed to God, that the one who mocks all good things might not have the joy of victory in that building. And so, while they knelt, like Elijah and Elisha our holy bishop prayed and blessed the boy, and he recovered the breath of life. The physicians bound up his broken limbs with bandages, and day by day his condition improved. He is still alive, his name is Bothelm, and he gives thanks to God.

The model for Wilfrid's miracle here is the story in Acts 20, where Eutychus falls from a window in Troas and is picked up dead, but is restored to life by Paul. Paul goes on with his teaching, not distracted by the mishap, just as the building of the church at Hexham goes on. Similar miracles are recorded of another great builder and politician in the later Anglo-Saxon period, St Æthelwold.

MISSION AND RELIEF WORK

Bede knew Eddius's work but he does not record this story. He, like Pope Gregory, had reservations about certain miracle stories, especially raisings of the dead. He also knew Bishop Wilfrid, and may have had reservations, too, about the character and learning of the great man: Wilfrid had given credence to someone who had ignorantly accused Bede of heresy. But Bede nevertheless gives an infinitely better account of Wilfrid's mission to the South Saxons than Eddius. Sussex was cut off from the rest of Anglo-Saxon England by the dense forest of the Weald, and was the last part of England to be converted. Bede's picture of the terrible despair of the people, alleviated by the missionary bishop, is one that sticks in the memory.

> By preaching to this nation, Bishop Wilfrid not only rescued them from the misery of perpetual damnation but also from unspeakable destruction and terrible death on earth. For three years before his coming to the kingdom, no rain had fallen in the area, and as a result a most severe famine mercilessly struck down the people. Often, it is said, 40 or 50 starving people would go to some cliff or sea shore, and holding hands together in their misery,

they would leap off, to fall to their deaths or die by drowning. But on the very same day that the people received the baptism of faith, gentle but ample rain fell and restored the earth, bringing back the greenery of the fields, and giving a happy and fruitful harvest. Having rejected their former superstition and renounced their idolatry, 'the heart and flesh of all cried out for the living God', and they understood that he who is the true God had granted them both inward and outward blessings by his heavenly grace.

For when Wilfrid first came to the kingdom, and saw the suffering and famine there, he taught them how to find food by fishing; for both the sea and their rivers were full of fish, but the people only knew how to fish for eels. So the bishop's men gathered up eel-nets from all around and threw them into the sea. And with the help of divine grace, they quickly caught 300 fish of various kinds. These were divided into three: 100 were given to the poor; 100 to the people from whom the nets had been borrowed; and 100 were kept for their own use. By this good deed the bishop gained the affection of them all, and they more willingly began to set their hope on heaven as preached by him, since they had received material benefit by his help.

The saint here works in close co-operation with God. When the people receive the water of baptism they also receive the rain they need for their crops from God. And just as God provides for their needs in the way only he can, so Wilfrid provides for the needs of the people in the way he can. It is possible that Bede's source for this story insisted on the slightly implausible notion that the people caught eels but did not know how to catch fish. But Bede clearly invokes the miraculous catch of fish in John 21, and Eddius mentions a similar miracle when Wilfrid goes to preach in Frisia. An interesting point here, though, is that Wilfrid foreshadows the modern missionary and aid movements, as he introduces new technology which enables the people to provide for themselves. And by showing he cares for their physical needs, he earns their trust in teaching them about their spiritual needs.

MIRACULOUS HOSPITALITY

The stories of Wilfrid give good examples of the active saintly life. Another of the dynamic saints was Æthelwold, one of the leaders of the movement in the 10th century that restored monasticism after the attacks of the Vikings. Æthelwold rebuilt the monastery at Abingdon, and on one occasion King Eadred came to see how the building was going. Now Æthelwold was a hospitable man, but an unexpected visit from the king must have caught him unawares.

> The abbot [Æthelwold] invited the king to dine with them in the guesthouse, and the king instantly accepted. It happened that the king had with him not a few thanes of Northumbrian origin, who went with him to the feast. The king was well pleased and ordered generous toasts of friendship in mead, and the doors were carefully locked so that nobody should escape and be seen to leave the royal feast. What more is to be said? The waiters drew the drink all day to the satisfaction of all those feasting, but the supply of drink in the

vessel did not fall below a handbreadth. The Northumbrians as usual became drunk, and left in the evening very merry.

This miracle is based on the story of the wedding at Cana in Galilee in John 2, where Jesus supplies the wine for a feast by changing water into wine; and also on the miracle of Elijah and the widow of Zarephath in 1 Kings 17, where the widow's oil does not run out no matter how much she uses. What is at stake in this story of Æthelwold is the monastery's reputation and possibly also the king's friendship and support. The writer, Wulfstan of Winchester, makes it fairly clear that he does not approve of the behaviour of the king's thanes, with his jibe about Northumbrians; and indeed the king seems a little too ready to accept Æthelwold's offer and a little too free with his host's mead. The next chapter mentions that the king died very soon after, and the much more religious King Edgar succeeded. But the miracle saved the day for Æthelwold, and everybody was pleased.

SPIRITUAL BATTLE

The more contemplative saints often have visions and temptations by demons. These are modelled at least to some extent on the temptation of Jesus in the wilderness in Matthew 4, but they take the idea much further than scripture. St Guthlac's *Life* has a very long chapter devoted to his experiences as evil spirits carry him to the gates of hell. As Guthlac is praying, his cell fills with clouds of demons:

[The foul spirits] were ghastly in appearance, terrible in shape with huge heads, long necks, narrow faces, pallid complexions, dirty beards, hairy ears, grim foreheads, ghastly eyes, foul-smelling mouths, horses' teeth, throats spewing out flames, crooked jaws, thick lips, dreadful voices, singed hair, bloated cheeks, pointed chests, mangy thighs, knobbly knees, crooked legs, swollen ankles, splay feet, wide-open mouths, hoarse shouts.

The demons are described in gruesome detail from head to foot. This is a virtuoso performance even by the standards of the genre, and the Anglo-Saxon audience would be in no doubt that Guthlac's experience was not a pleasant one. But he is rescued by St Bartholomew and a band of angels who carry him swiftly to safety. And before they disappear in a puff of smoke, two demons bitterly tell Guthlac that they have met their match in him.

OPPOSITION

Guthlac is also one of many saints who encounter bitter opposition from those who would be expected to support and indeed admire them. All is not necessarily sweetness and light, even among monks and clergy. Poison is one preferred method of trying to do away with the saint. Æthelwold aroused the hostility of the secular clergy whom he ousted from the Old Minster at Winchester in order to make it a regular monastic house. They put poison in his drink, and aware of its deadly effect on him, Æthelwold musters his faith by quoting Mark 16:18 to himself, and miraculously escapes harm.

The attempt on Guthlac's life is less cunning:

There was a certain cleric called Beccel who volunteered to be the servant of such a great man, and offered to live in purity for God under his guidance. But an evil spirit came into his heart and began to inflame him with destructive vainglory and pride. And when his swollen and vain pride had seduced him with its arrogance, he also began to encourage him to take a lethal sword and kill the master under whose guidance he had started to live for God. The devil put it into his mind that if he could kill Guthlac, he would be able to live afterwards in his place, and would have the greatest veneration of kings and princes.

So, on a certain day when the aforementioned cleric came to Guthlac the man of God, as he usually did every 20 days, in order to tonsure him, he was seized with a great madness, and thirsting with overwhelming lust for the blood of the man of God, he advanced intending to kill him. Then the saint of God, Guthlac, to whom the Lord constantly revealed foreknowledge of things to come, aware of this new sinful crime, began to question him: 'O my Beccel, why do you hide the ancient enemy in your foolish heart? Why do you not spit out the lethal drink of bitter poison? I know you have been taken in by an evil spirit. So then, turning away from them, confess the disgraceful thoughts that the hostile enemy of humankind has put into your mind.' When Beccel realized that he had been seduced by an evil spirit, he prostrated himself before the feet of the great man Guthlac, with tearful voice he confessed his offence, and humbly prayed for pardon. The man of blessed memory, Guthlac, not only forgave his fault but also promised that in future troubles he would come to Beccel's assistance.

Æthelwold forgave his poisoners, and Guthlac sees that Beccel was suffering the delusions of the devil. His gentleness and kindness to the man, and promise of future help, prepare the way for the veneration of his relics, by which that help will come to others.

MIRACLES AT THE SHRINE

All kinds of miracles are possible at the tomb or shrine of the saint. Bede tells the story of the Northumbrian King Oswald, who died in battle against marauding Celts and Mercians. But because Oswald was a Christian king, working with the missionary Aidan in converting his people, and because he did all kinds of good deeds, his bones work miracles, proving his sanctity. The monastery at Bardney in Lincolnshire hesitates to receive his bones, but a mysterious light shines over them at night, and the monks are convinced. In the Old English version by Ælfric, the story goes on:

> Then the holy bones were washed and carried into the church and they laid them out reverently in a shrine. And many people who were ill were healed of various diseases by his holy merits. The water that the bones were washed with inside the church had been poured away as it were in a corner, and the earth on which the water fell afterwards became a remedy for many. Devils were put to flight from people, who were earlier afflicted with madness, by the dust. Likewise, where he fell slain in battle, people took the earth to those who were ill, and put it into water for the sick to drink, and they were healed by the holy man...
> Now the holy man Bede, who wrote this book,

says it is no wonder that the holy king heals illness when he lives in heaven, because he wanted to help those who were poor and weak and give them sustenance when he was alive here. Now he has honour with Almighty God in the eternal realm because of his goodness.

It is not only people who are healed: horses are, too, and a beam of a house in a fire remains unburnt because some of the earth from where the saintly king died has been hung in a bag on it. Bede notes that a pit about six feet deep was excavated because people wanted the healing power of the earth.

The fascination with relics of the dead strikes the modern reader as bizarre. But the point of these stories is that it reinforces the orthodox Christian view that death is not the end, but rather the perfecting of the human being; and that earth is a preparation for heaven. Here both Bede and Ælfric make the connection between what the saint did when he lived, and what he still does, more powerfully, as one of God's agents after his earthly death. The Anglo-Saxons knew that the world was beset with evil spirits. They were glad that both earth and heaven were populated by the saints, for the saints were those who had overcome the devil by devotion to Christ. The saints were the tokens of God's victory in the spiritual battle.

A Latin hymn for All Saints, 1 November

1. The feast day of All Saints is celebrated in all the world, the day of those who reign happily in the heavenly regions together with you, O Jesus.

2. It is these we invoke with bowed heads and it is also you, redeemer of all. As suppliants we address prayers to them and to you, sighing the while.

3. Jesus, saviour of the world, assist and aid those whom you redeemed and you, loving mother of God, demand salvation for the wretched.

4. May all the hosts of the angels and the troops of the patriarchs and the prophets by virtue of their merits pray for forgiveness unto us.

5. May the Baptist who preceded Christ and the bearer of the key to heaven release us from the bond of sin in concert with the other apostles.

6. May the holy choir of martyrs and the priests by virtue of their being confessors and the maidens by virtue of their chastity purify us of our transgressions.

7. May the intercession of the monks and may all citizens of heaven grant the requests of the suppliants and ask the reward of life for them.

8. Praise, honour, might and glory be to God, the Father and the Son together with the Holy Ghost in eternity.

Not everyone feels at home with the idea of the intercession of the saints. But the Anglo-Saxons felt that the enterprise of salvation, while effected uniquely by Christ, was nevertheless an intensely corporate affair. Those who had gone before were interested in the salvation of people in the world, and when people practised the virtues which the saints were renowned for, the saints were somehow involved.

8

ST CUTHBERT

HISTORY

 We have looked at saints in general, now we turn to one particular Anglo-Saxon saint, Cuthbert. St Cuthbert was one of the greatest saints of Anglo-Saxon England. He reached full maturity and prominence in challenging times for the Church in England. He grew up as Northumbria was converting to Christianity, and he became a leader in the Northumbrian church as it faced a dispute over the dating of Easter and other practices. He was influential in his life and teaching as the dust settled on that dispute, and after his death his influence continued through his prophecies and relics as a patron of the Church in the following centuries.

The details of his life are sometimes a little obscure, but he was apparently born sometime around 635 in the kingdom of Northumbria. He decided to enter a monastery in 651, after seeing a vision. As a monk he travelled the length and breadth of the kingdom of Northumbria preaching and ministering among the people. For several years before 685, he was a hermit on St Cuthbert's Island, near Lindisfarne, where he was visited by many because of his fame. In 685 he was persuaded to become a bishop, and for two years held the see of Lindisfarne. He died on 20 March 687, having retired to his island hermitage knowing of his approaching death. In 698 his body was moved to Lindisfarne so that it could be given greater honour, and it was found to be perfect and unaffected by decay. Many miracles were said to be performed by the saint and his relics.

LIVES AND ACCOUNTS OF THE SAINT

This bare outline of St Cuthbert's life and death gives little indication of what it was that made him famous and so attractive to the Anglo-Saxons. Two writers wrote about Cuthbert's life, in Latin, at a time when stories were being told about him by people who had seen the events or been touched by Cuthbert himself. These were an anonymous monk of Lindisfarne, who wrote his *Life of St Cuthbert* either in the last year of the seventh century or very early in the eighth; and Bede, who modified the anonymous writer's *Life* first in verse, then later in prose. Bede's prose *Life* was written a decade or more after the anonymous writer's, sometime between 710 and 720.

Bede also wrote a brief account of Cuthbert in his *Ecclesiastical History*, in 731, and this is where we will begin.

In the same year that he died, King Ecgfrith had the holy and venerable man Cuthbert consecrated as bishop of Lindisfarne ... Cuthbert had been living a solitary life in great mental and physical austerity for many years on a small island in the ocean called Farne, about nine miles away from Lindisfarne church. From the time of his earliest childhood he had always wanted to live as a monk, but when he became a young man he took the habit and name. He first entered the monastery of Melrose which is on the banks of the Tweed, and was then ruled by Abbot Eata. Eata was the gentlest, most uncomplicated of men and was afterwards made bishop of Hexham or Lindisfarne ... The prior at that time was Boisil, a priest with great virtues and a spirit of prophecy. Cuthbert humbly submitted to Boisil's teaching and gained from him knowledge of the scriptures and a model of good deeds.

Cuthbert was a remarkable man, with a clear sense of vocation even from earliest childhood. But even such people need to be trained and taught, and the two men mentioned in this paragraph, Eata and Boisil, have precisely those gifts which Cuthbert later demonstrated in their highest state of development: gentleness and a prophetic spirit. Even saintly gifts are ones that can be modelled, informed by the scriptures, and taught by those who remain obscure and remote from fame in the world. Bede goes on to show how Cuthbert balanced his desire for the monastic, and indeed hermit, life with concern for those around him.

When Boisil departed to be with the Lord, Cuthbert was made prior of the monastery. By his authority as a teacher, and by the example of his own deeds, he trained many in the regular monastic life. But he not only taught and gave an example of how to live under the Rule in the monastery. More than that, he took pains to convert the surrounding people, both far and near, from foolish habits to a love for the joys of heaven. Many indeed profaned the faith they held by wicked deeds; and some in times of plague had reverted to the false remedies of idolatry, turning away from the sacraments of the faith into which they had been baptized, as if incantations and amulets or other such secret devilish devices could be any use against a calamity sent by the creator God.

So he often went out of the monastery to put right both these errors, sometimes on horseback, but more often on foot. Just as Boisil had done earlier, he went to the surrounding villages and preached the true way of life to those who had gone astray. It was customary at that time among the English that whenever a priest or cleric came to the village, at his order everyone would gather to hear the Word. They would gladly listen to what was said and even more gladly follow what they heard and could understand in what they did. Cuthbert's skill in speaking was so great, his love of pressing home his message so evident, and such was the angelic brightness of his face, that none of those present dared conceal from him the secrets of their hearts. Rather, they all openly confessed the things they had done wrong, because they all believed that these things could never be hidden completely from him. And, as he ordered them, they washed away the sins they confessed by 'fruits worthy of repentance'.

He used to go to preach in villages especially in those places in steep and inhospitable mountain country which others feared to visit, and where the poverty and barbarity of the people kept teachers away. He devoted himself gladly to this pious labour, and so carefully and persistently taught them that having left the monastery he would often not return home for a whole week, or sometimes two or three, even on occasion for a whole month. He would stay among the peasants of the hill-country, calling them to heavenly things by the words of his preaching and his good works.

Cuthbert had a unique collection of gifts which often must have required of him hard decisions. He had longed to live in a monastery under the Rule since early childhood, yet he loved ordinary people so much he could hardly drag himself away from them. He was humble and earnest and innocent, yet he had power in his speech and authority in his manner. He had responsibility in the monastery, but saw the monastery as a means to the end of building up the kingdom of God by teaching the people outside it. He was gentle and persistent, caring and clear-sighted.

INTEGRITY OF LIFE AND TEACHING

Perhaps the aspect of Cuthbert's character that Bede most wants his readers to understand here, is that Cuthbert's life matched his teaching. He practised what he preached. In this time of great expansion in the Church and conversion of the nobility, there was a risk, and more than a risk, that people would be carried along by enthusiasm but then left to fend for themselves. Bede notes that some who had been baptized would apostasize in times of plague, and others simply did not change their lifestyle at all, but were baptized because it was the done thing. Their lives did not match their Christian profession, and Cuthbert set himself to remedy ignorance, to rebuke and teach, to encourage and love the people that others had abandoned. And to do it by word and deed, as in fact Boisil had done before him.

Bede tells us that Eata later transferred Cuthbert to Lindisfarne, where he also encouraged the monks for many years. Once again, he 'taught the brothers with the authority of the prior and modelled his teaching in his own actions'. This habitual practice of carrying out his own precepts equipped Cuthbert to move next into the life of the hermit. By preaching and teaching, he had earned the right to silence. He settled on his barren little island, and was miraculously provided with food and fresh water.

> And so for many years he served God in solitude
> in that place, and the rampart surrounding his
> dwelling was so high that he could see nothing but
> the heavens which he yearned to enter from it . . .
> A great synod . . . over which Archbishop
> Theodore of blessed memory presided, unani-
> mously elected Cuthbert to the see of the church
> of Lindisfarne. But though many letters and mes-
> sengers were sent to him, nothing could uproot
> him from his monastery. Eventually the king,
> Ecgfrith himself, and the most holy Bishop
> Trumwine, along with many other religious and
> powerful men, sailed to the island. Many of the
> brothers from the island of Lindisfarne also came
> on the same errand, and all kneeling, with tears
> flowing, they appealed to him in the name of the
> Lord. At last they brought him, also in tears, out of
> his beloved hiding-place, and took him forcibly to
> the synod. Once there, and despite his reluctance,
> he was overcome by their unanimous wish and was
> compelled to undertake the duty of the bishopric. . .

When he had been consecrated bishop, his good deeds after the pattern of the blessed apostles adorned the episcopal office. He protected the people committed to his care by constant prayers and called them to heavenly things by his helpful teachings. And, as is the habit of the best teachers, what he taught them to do, he first did himself. He was above all fired with divine love, patient and disciplined, persistent and urgent in prayerful devotion, and kindly to all who came to him for comfort. He believed that giving weak brethren help and advice was as good as prayer. . .

After two years, Cuthbert retired again to his island hermitage and died there. It was customary for people elected bishop to protest their unworthiness, but Cuthbert was evidently more than usually reluctant. He longed for heaven, but once compelled to take the office of bishop, he helped others to long for heaven. And he seems to have done it by teaching and example in which there was a strong element of practicality. His view might have been, to modify a phrase, 'a little help is worth a great deal of prayer', without in the least diminishing the importance of the devotion which shaped and rooted his life in God.

THE TRADITIONS OF THE SAINT: CHILDHOOD AND YOUTH

This account given by Bede of Cuthbert's life leaves out a great deal of the tradition, because (as Bede explains) the stories about the saint had been written at length elsewhere in the various versions of the *Life of St Cuthbert*. Lives of this sort follow patterns, as we have seen already. But within the conventional patterns of Cuthbert's *Lives*, a real character can be discerned; whether or not we believe the stories as historical fact, they show how people who knew him felt that he helped them.

Bede notes Cuthbert's sense of vocation in passing, above. But the *Lives* show how this was developed. As a boy, spending time playing games and wrestling, Cuthbert is addressed as 'most holy priest and bishop' and rebuked by a three-year-old for behaviour unsuited to his high office. Thus he is marked out by God for his future role. He is also given a recipe to cure a tumour of the knee by a passing angelic horseman, one of a series of ministrations by angels by which Cuthbert is supported and equipped for the rigours of his life.

Bede inserts a story at this point which shows Cuthbert's courage, and his precocious desire to preach and teach. Cuthbert is still a young man, not yet a monk. As one of a crowd, he sees some monks on rafts near the mouth of the Tyne being driven off course by contrary winds, and in danger of being lost at sea.

> The crowd began to jeer at their way of common life, as if anyone were deserving of this kind of suffering for spurning the ordinary usages of human beings and introducing new and strange rules of living. Cuthbert put a stop to the abuse of the mockers, saying, 'What are you doing, brothers, slandering people who are even now being carried off to destruction? Wouldn't it be better and more humane to pray to the Lord for them to be saved rather than finding pleasure in their perils?' But, crude in mind and words, they contradicted him, 'No one should plead for them, and God should

not have mercy on them, because they have taken away the old ways of worship, and nobody knows how the new worship should be carried out.' When he got this response, Cuthbert knelt down with his head bowed to the ground, and prayed to God, and immediately the strong wind shifted and blew the rafts undamaged back to land . . . Seeing this, the people were embarrassed at their unbelief.

Cuthbert stands, and indeed kneels, as one of the crowd. The people are shown as ignorant, fearful, and resentful of the monks who represent the new ways and who set themselves apart. What Cuthbert does here is what he does throughout most of his life: he speaks as one of the people, addressing them as 'brothers', but with knowledge and compassion and a clear faith in God. He shows the crowd how the 'new worship' should be carried out simply by praying. And the people respond to him in his unaffected goodness.

MONASTIC LIFE

A decisive moment for Cuthbert is when he decides to become a monk. When watching sheep one night, he sees a vision of light in which a soul is received into heaven. The loveliness of the vision makes him start to yearn for heaven himself. He finds out that Aidan, the great Irish bishop and missionary to the Northumbrians, had died at the time he saw the vision, and at once decides to enter a monastery. The anonymous *Life* interprets this experience as a spiritual vision such as Jacob saw at Bethel in Genesis 28:12, a turning-point in Jacob's life. But though he does not explicitly say so, Bede sees it as something more like the experience of the shepherds on the hillside at the birth of Jesus, with a heavenly choir.

And, like those shepherds, Cuthbert leaves the sheep and goes to find what gift God has for him by entering a monastery.

Bede's observations on the progress of Cuthbert's life in the monasteries have already been mentioned. During his time at Melrose, when he travelled about, he became deeply attached to a man called Hildmer and his wife, and this led to an opportunity for him to help them.

There was a high officer of King Ecgfrith called Hildmer. This man, and all his household, was very dedicated in performing good spiritual works. For this reason saintly Cuthbert loved him especially, and when he was travelling in that direction frequently called in. Hildmer's wife busied herself with charitable deeds and other good works. But for all this, she was suddenly seized by a demon and began to be most bitterly tormented. She gnashed her teeth and let out wretched cries. In her frenzy she threw her arms and legs about, and all who saw or heard her were greatly horrified. After the seizure she lay spent and seemed to be on the verge of death.

So her husband got on his horse and rode flat out to the man of God. And he begged him, 'My wife is ill and seems to be on the verge of death. Please send a priest to attend her before she dies, to give her the sacrament of the body and blood of the Lord. And please let her body be buried here in holy ground.' He was ashamed to admit that she was insane, because the man of God had always seen her in her normal state.

Cuthbert left him for a while to see about a priest who could be sent with him. While he was doing this, the realization dawned in his spirit that it was not an ordinary illness, but a demonic oppression that the wife was suffering from. And this was why Hildmer had begged help for her. Cuthbert turned back to him and said, 'I must come with you to visit her. I won't send someone else.'

On the way there the man began to cry, and the tears running down his cheeks showed the misery of his heart. He was afraid that when Cuthbert found she was demon-possessed, he would form the opinion that she had not served the Lord with true faith, but had been pretending. But the man of God gently comforted him, saying, 'Don't cry. We won't find your wife in a state that will upset me to see. Although you are ashamed to say it, I know well that she is tormented by a demon. But I also know that before we even reach her, the demon will be banished. She will be freed, and as we arrive she will joyfully run out to meet us. She will take these reins, perfectly sound of mind, and quickly inviting us to come in, she will carefully look after us as usual. It isn't only bad people who are exposed to such suffering. But according to the mysterious decision of God, sometimes the innocent in this world are seized not only in body, but also in mind, by the devil.'

By the time Cuthbert had finished speaking these and similar words for Hildmer's comfort and instruction, they were near the house. As they came, the demon suddenly fled, unable to bear the approach of the Holy Spirit who filled the man of God. The woman was freed from her bondage, and immediately got up as if she had been woken up from a deep sleep. She ran to welcome the man of God, and took the bridle of the horse on which he was sitting. Then, in full possession of vigour of body and mind, she begged Cuthbert to dismount swiftly and to bless her home by going in. She offered him devoted care, and plainly declared how, at the first touch of his horse's bridle, she sensed that she had been completely freed from all the trouble of her old attacks.

Bede tells the story well. We feel the distress and misery of Hildmer, his fear that Cuthbert will misinterpret the ugly symptoms of his wife's illness. And we see very clearly the love and care of Cuthbert for Hildmer and his wife. Some manuscripts of the *Life* add the woman's name, Eadswith, but Bede either did not know it, or wanted to protect her memory. Cuthbert brings reassurance to Hildmer and healing to Eadswith, recognizing that illness affects body, mind and spirit. And strikingly, it is Cuthbert's presence that brings about the healing: he does no more than be there, and foresee the outcome. The power of the Holy Spirit gives impact to the twofold ministry that Cuthbert has habitually practised: teaching and going among the people. And characteristically Cuthbert sees the real problem and its resolution through the 'spirit of prophecy'.

The story follows two biblical patterns. In Luke 4:38–9, Jesus heals Peter's mother-in-law, and she gets up from her bed and serves him, just as Eadswith looks after Cuthbert when she has been healed. But important as this is, there is another pattern that is equally significant. Hildmer was worried that people would think Eadswith could not be a real Christian if she was afflicted in this horrible way. He was even worried that she would not be allowed a Christian burial because of her problem. So Cuthbert's teaching and comfort to Hildmer follows the pattern of Jesus when he healed the deformed woman in Luke 13:10–17. In verse 16, Jesus refers to the woman as a 'daughter of Abraham' – a woman of faith – but she has nevertheless been 'bound by Satan for 18 long years'. So innocent Eadswith's 'old attacks' come from spiritual oppression. Cuthbert brings Eadswith and Hildmer to a better understanding of spiritual mysteries, but he also demonstrates the power of God to help.

THE HERMIT

In due course, Cuthbert was moved to Lindisfarne, and started to long for the hermit life. After some time his wish was granted, and he set up his hermitage on the island of Farne, and worked to support himself. The barren little island produced enough for him to live on, and he had at this stage a regular flow of visitors, for whom a lodging house was built. But some birds had their eyes on the thatch.

> One particular day, Cuthbert was digging and making trenches in the earth on his island. For two or three years early on [in his life as a hermit], he worked daily and got his food by the work of his hands. For he knew the saying, 'whoever does not work, shall not eat'. This was before he shut himself away inside closed doors.
>
> While he was digging, he saw two ravens which had been in that place for a long time. They were destroying the roof of the house built for those who visited by sea, near the harbour, and making their nest with the thatch. With a gentle movement of

his hand he tried to keep them from doing this harm to the brothers of the monastery in building their nest. But they ignored him. In the end he became annoyed, and warning them severely in the name of Jesus Christ to leave the island, he drove them away. Immediately, without delay and just as he commanded, they left their home.

But after three days, one of the two birds came back to the feet of the man of God as he was digging the earth. It landed on top of the furrow. Spreading its wings and bowing its head, with a humble voice it began to croak, begging forgiveness and grace. The servant of God understood that they were sorry, and allowed them to come back. As soon as this settlement was reached, the ravens both returned to the island. As a little gift, each had in its beak about half a piece of pig lard which it brought to Cuthbert's feet. He forgave them their sin, and they are still there on the island to this day. This story was related to me by most reliable witnesses, who when they visited Cuthbert greased their boots with the lard over the course of a full year, praising God.

This story is as it is told in the anonymous *Life of Saint Cuthbert*, and it is one that is better told by the anonymous author than by Bede. Animal stories of this kind were common in the Celtic tradition, from which the anonymous *Life* comes. They show a delight in the natural world and a sense of kinship with it. One of the repeated patterns in the Celtic lives of the saints is that through their holiness and closeness to God, saints are able to be at one with the world around them. They have power over it without having to resort to force. So the animals and birds help the saint in his or her mission.

Often the animal stories reinforce a moral which has its human counterpart. The story of St Cuthbert and the otters has been mentioned already. Just as the otters humbly prostrate themselves before the saint's feet as they warm them, so, as Cuthbert returns to the monastery, does the man who illicitly watched the saint throw himself at the saint's feet asking for forgiveness. In this story of the ravens, the birds at first ignore the saint, but then have to obey. And in the same way, in a story recorded by Bede, Cuthbert casually advises some visitors to cook and eat a goose before sailing away. As they have their own food, they do not bother, and a storm blows up and keeps them on the island for a whole week until they complain to Cuthbert, who casually notes that the goose is still uncooked. As soon as the saint is obeyed, the storm dies down, and the visitors are able to leave, somewhat ashamed, but the wiser for their experience. The point is perhaps that obedience can be willing or enforced: human beings can learn from the natural world that willing obedience is better.

This story of the ravens would have had more point for the Anglo-Saxons because the raven was a fearful bird. In Old English poetry it was, with the wolf and eagle, one of the deadly trio of animals that feasted on the slain after battle. It is sometimes called 'the hard-beaked one', and was known to be savagely greedy. The humble repentance of the birds in the story, and the way they use their once-terrible beaks to bring a little gift to Cuthbert, shows the power of holiness to transform and remake the world.

BISHOP OF LINDISFARNE

Cuthbert plays his part in politics as bishop of Lindisfarne. He advises the king and visits the people in times of trouble and plague. He predicts the king's death, and in due course his own. In Northumbria, powerful people were not only found in the secular world of the court, but also in the monasteries. Bede is strongly critical of monasteries which were merely extensions of secular power, without the heart and life of true monasticism. So when he mentions Verca, abbess of South Shields, as one of 'highest nobility in worldly terms', he is perhaps alerting the reader to some reservations about the monastery in this regard. At any rate, he makes clear that the real power belongs to Cuthbert in this story:

> Cuthbert arrived at the monastery of virgins not far from the mouth of the River Tyne, where he was splendidly received by Abbess Verca. She was a devout handmaid of Christ, and in worldly terms of the highest nobility. After he had got up from the midday rest, he said that he was thirsty and asked for a drink. They asked what he would like to drink, and requested to be allowed to bring him wine or beer. 'Give me water,' he said. They brought him water drawn from the well. When he had blessed it and drunk a small quantity, he gave it to his attendant priest, who passed it on to a servant. When the servant had taken the cup he said, 'Am I allowed to drink from the cup from which the bishop has drunk?' He answered, 'Of course; why not?' This man was a priest of the same monastery. So he drank, and it appeared to him that the water had changed so that it tasted like

wine. And desiring to add to his own witness to so great a miracle, he passed the cup to a brother who was standing nearby. When he, too, had drunk from it, he tasted wine in his mouth instead of water. They looked at each other in wonder. And when they had a spare moment to talk, they confessed to each other that they had never drunk better wine as it seemed to them. This miracle is told just as one of them afterwards related it me: he lived for no short time in our monastery which is at the mouth of the River Wear, and where he now lies peacefully buried.

Jesus turned water into wine for a wedding feast in John 2. Bede actually avoids claiming that the water in this story was made into wine by Cuthbert, asserting rather that it *tasted* like it. But the rationale for the miracle at Cana by Jesus is given as 'he thus revealed his glory', and it is perhaps not too far from Bede's mind that Cuthbert was following his divine Master in this, and giving an example to those present of spiritual power as distinct from secular power.

DEATH

After a full ministry of two years, and knowing that he is about to die, Cuthbert returns to his island. The chapters in the anonymous *Life* dealing with these events are brief. Of Cuthbert's death, the anonymous writer simply records, 'After Bishop Cuthbert of holy memory had taken communion, he lifted up his eyes and hands to heaven, and commending his soul to the Lord, he gave up his spirit'.

But Bede has much more to say. For him, Cuthbert was one who resolved in his own life the tensions which the Church of the time faced. Cuthbert was fired by desire for the monastic life by the vision of St Aidan, the Irish missionary bishop. But in later life, Cuthbert encountered hostility from the monks at Lindisfarne when he tried to teach and establish them in the ways of the Roman church which the Anglo-Saxons had adopted after the council of Whitby in 664. Bede thought the Celtic ways were wrong, and has Cuthbert say so on his death-bed.

> He said, 'Always maintain peace and divine love between yourselves ... And also keep concord with other servants of Christ ... by no means deeming yourselves better than others in the same faith and life. But with those who err from the unity of catholic peace, whether in not celebrating Easter at the right time, or in lives of perversity, let there be no communion. And be aware and keep it in memory that if you have to choose between two evils, I would much rather that you took my bones from the tomb, and carried them with you away from this place, and lived wherever God might provide, than that you should agree to iniquity and put your necks to the yoke of schismatics...'

There are echoes of the real St Cuthbert here: the humility, the eirenical spirit, and indeed the spirit of prophecy. But it is Bede's passion for orthodoxy that slips in the reference to celebrating Easter at the right time, and to 'schismatics', because this was one of the major tensions between the Celtic and Roman branches of the Church in England, and one with which Bede was particularly preoccupied.

HELP FOR THE OPPRESSED

What Cuthbert, Bede or any of the contemporary audience could not have known, except by the spirit of prophecy, was that St Cuthbert's community did have to face two evils two centuries later. In the Viking attacks of the later ninth century, monastic life at Lindisfarne became impossible because of constant raids and disruption. The monks who remained were left with a terrible dilemma: either to abandon the monastic life altogether, or to travel about taking Cuthbert's bones from the tomb with them, along with the other things that remained to them as a monastic community. Hungry and oppressed, the faithful few put Cuthbert's relics on a cart and wandered around, just as Cuthbert predicted, looking for the place God would provide for them. Thinking that that place might be in Ireland, they tried to escape the attentions of the Vikings by sailing there. On this occasion, a storm prevented them getting across the sea, and to their grief washed overboard the gospel-book which was one of their remaining treasures. Symeon of Durham tells the story of how St Cuthbert saved the day, saved the community, and saved the gospel-book, which we now know as the Lindisfarne Gospels.

[St Cuthbert] appeared in a vision to ... Hunred, and commanded that when the tide had gone out they should look for the book which (as was mentioned earlier) had fallen out of the ship among the waves, and perhaps contrary to anything they could hope for, they would by God's mercy find it. The loss of this book had indeed disturbed their minds with the greatest sadness. St Cuthbert also added to these words the following: 'Get up at once and show the bridle, which you will see hanging from a tree, to the horse which you will find not far from here, and it will immediately come to you of its own accord and you should take care to bridle it. Then with the horse pulling the cart on which my body is carried about, you will be able to follow it with less effort.' Grasping these instructions, Hunred immediately roused up from sleep, and told the vision he had seen and soon sent several of the brothers to the sea nearby to look for the book which they had lost. Now at this time they had arrived at a place called the White House, or by the common people, Whithorn.

So they went to the sea and discovered that it had receded much farther than normal. And when they had walked out three miles or more, they found that same holy book of the gospels, which retained its cover of rich jewels and gold, and inside revealed the original beauty of its letters and pages, as if it had not been touched by the water at all. This lifted up their troubled minds with no small measure of joy, and it was impossible to doubt the aforementioned man in the matter of the other things he had heard. Going on, he found the bridle hanging from a tree, as he had been told in his dream; and then looking around, he saw a little way off a horse of reddish colour. Where it had come from and how it came to be in that lonely place he could not at all imagine. When he raised his hand and showed it the bridle, as he had been commanded, the horse came quickly to him and allowed itself to be bridled at his hands. When he had led it to his brothers, they rejoiced to labour afterwards all the more on behalf of the body of father Cuthbert, when they knew for certain that his support would never fail them in their need. Harnessing the horse to the vehicle on which they carried that heavenly treasure enclosed in a chest, they followed it more confidently wherever it went because they were using the horse provided to guide them by God.

In the end it was not 'schismatics' that threatened the Church and the community of St Cuthbert, but the ravages of the Vikings. And the presence and help of their patron was one of the things that kept them going.

CUTHBERT

In the various accounts of St Cuthbert we can actually watch as the conventions of the saint's life are explored and the emphases of the stories change with the different writers. The anonymous writer has his preoccupations, and Bede has his. But some things remain constant. Cuthbert was a man of sympathy, power and vision. In the simplicity and devotion of his life he inspired and touched and encouraged people. Perhaps at the root of his fascination for his contemporaries and those who read his stories today, is the fact that he conquered self. And in a curiously paradoxical way, this meant that he was more individual, more himself, than others. Whatever actually happened with the Lindisfarne Gospels, we might perhaps feel that it would be *just like* Cuthbert to ensure that they were preserved undamaged to delight and teach and enrich his poor oppressed community, and generations to come.

A Latin hymn for the feast of St Cuthbert, 20 March

1. The great and admirable soldier who shines forth through his many merits, Cuthbert, now enjoys his eternal reward with the Lord.
2. He crushed the fires of the flesh, for in his heart he had faith in the Lord and so despised everything transitory in his duty to charity.
3. Joyfully he fulfilled the commands of the law of the Lord in his works. Generous, eager, a giver of light, he was praised for his merits.
4. He caused a stream to spring, a sign in perpetuity, to flow where no traces of a spring were before to be seen.
5. He released a tongue from its ties which had been paralysed for a long time. In a short time he brought forth a crop from the rocky soil.
6. We pray for his continual help so that we may deserve to say joyfully without end:
7. 'Glory be to the unbegotten Father, glory to the Only-begotten together with the Holy Ghost throughout all the ages.'

This hymn is from the Durham Hymnal, and it gives a highly abbreviated version of Cuthbert's life, including a number of miracles which have not been quoted at length above. It remembers Cuthbert's severity towards himself in verse 2, before dwelling at greater length on his overflowing creativity, which defied the limits of time and place. As is appropriate for a place which has close ties to the man, it celebrates his feast with genuine exuberance.

9

MARTYRS

Martyrs are different from saints in that their death, and what immediately precedes it, is the main focus of attention. Saints die piously, usually with instructive words and praise to God on their lips. But it is their lives of devotion that give them their power, and the miracles performed by their relics tend to be the kind of things that the living saint was in the habit of doing. Martyrs are often pious before their death but their power derives from the kind of death they die. Classically, it is their refusal to deny the faith that leads to their torture and death. But this is modified a little in Anglo-Saxon times, as we shall see.

The Anglo-Saxons inherited a full martyrology. The stories of the Christian martyrs who had died under the persecuting Roman emperors were well known. The frightful tortures endured by the martyrs must have given the Anglo-Saxons a certain thrill of horror as well as a sense of the power of God. The stories are pretty unashamedly graphic as well as pious, and their writers and tellers were well aware of the fascination as well as repulsiveness of the violence. Most martyr stories would not make films for universal viewing. But many, particularly the early stories, have a core of fact which is often as bizarre as the human imagination could invent. The Roman historian Tacitus tells us that the Emperor Nero had Christians torn to death by dogs, crucified, and burned alive as torches for his evening garden parties. Other historians tell similar stories. In due course, though, the martyrdoms were elaborated with fictional horrors and reprieves.

THE OLD ENGLISH MARTYROLOGY

In the Old English Martyrology, there are brief notices about martyrs and saints. St Eugenia had a stone tied around her neck and was thrown into the River Tiber, but floated; and was then thrown into an oven, but it cooled suddenly; and so she was starved. St John the Evangelist was forced to drink poison without dying. St Felix was put naked on sharp shells and stones, but was released from prison by an angel. St Sebastian was shot full of arrows without dying, and so was beaten to death with sticks. St Agnes was stripped and put in a brothel, but was not violated, until she was killed by being stabbed in the throat. Forty soldiers were thrown into an icy pool, while a hot bath steamed nearby for any who would renounce his faith. Each one of these was celebrated on the day of their death in the Christian calendar, which by the end of the Anglo-Saxon period was very full.

ST JULIANA

Women and children were martyred as well as men. Some aspects of martyrdom stories are particular to women, especially the threat of unwanted marriage and the corresponding threat to virgin purity. Virginity was very highly regarded by Anglo-Saxon Christians: they saw it as modelled by Jesus himself, recommended by St Paul, and as symbolizing the purity of the soul's desire for Christ. This aspect comes into play in the story of St Juliana, who was martyred under the Roman Emperor Maximian, who ruled for a time alongside Diocletian at the end of the third century and early in the fourth. Juliana was betrothed to a Roman senator, Eleusius, at the age of eight. When she was 18, Eleusius pressed for the wedding, but by this time she had become a Christian and refused to marry unless Eleusius also became a Christian. She was tortured and subsequently martyred.

The essential details of the martyrdom of St Juliana were known to Bede at the beginning of the eighth century. Some time later, a poet called Cynewulf, who identifies himself by weaving his name in runic letters into the end of his poems, made a version in Old English verse. Later, another poet told the story in Middle English verse. It was a popular story, and it illustrates many martyrdom conventions, as well as fitting neatly into the conventions of Old English heroic verse.

SETTING THE SCENE

The opening lines set the scene:

> Lo, we have heard heroes declare this,
> men bold in deeds proclaim it, what happened
>   in the days
> of Maximian, the wicked king,
> the one who throughout the world began
>   persecution,
> killed Christian people, razed churches,
> shed on the grassy fields the
> blood of holy God-worshippers
> and righteous people. His realm was extensive,

spacious and honoured above the nations,
almost covering the whole wide earth.
As he had commanded, his powerful thanes
went from town to town. Often they roused
    up violence,
men deluded in actions who hated the law of
    the Lord,
by wickedness roused up hatred,
exalted idolatry, tortured the saints,
destroyed the learned, burned the elect,
persecuted the warriors of God with spear and fire.
    There was a certain wealthy, powerful reeve
of noble birth. He ruled fortified towns
and constantly defended the land.
He kept his treasure in the city
called Nicomedia. He often went to the shrine,
very eagerly went to the idols
against God's word. He was known by the name of
Heliseus, and he had a great and glorious
province. Then his mind turned to love
for a virgin, Juliana,
and his desire tormented him. In her heart she had
holy faith, and she earnestly resolved
that she would preserve her pure virginity
free from sin for the love of Christ.
The virgin was pledged to the wealthy man
according to her father's wish. He did not know
    how things would turn out,
how she, the young woman, despised the
    suitor's love
in her heart. The fear of God
was greater in her thoughts than all the treasure
which remained among the possessions of the prince.

The wealthy man, the one rich in gold,
was then eager in his mind for the nuptials,
that the virgin should be made ready for him
as a bride for his home. She firmly resisted
the warrior's love, despite the fact that he
    possessed
earthly treasures under lock and key in hoards,
limitless jewels. She despised all that,
and said these words in the crowds of people:
'I can tell you that you do not need to
trouble yourself further. If you will love and trust
the true God, and lift up his praise,
and will acknowledge the Protector of souls, I will
    be ready
immediately and resolutely for your will.
Similarly, I tell you, if you will by your action
in idolatry trust in a worse god,
and promise heathen sacrifice, you will not be able
    to have me,
nor force me to be your companion.
You will never be able to prepare torment
    so powerful
through violent malice, nor sufferings so severe,
that you will turn me from these words.'

There is a tension in this story. It was custom for girls to do as
their fathers wished, and moreover to be deferential to their
social superiors and those who had wealth and power. Not
surprisingly, Juliana's public statement does not please
Heliseus. But Cynewulf shows that Juliana is in fact being
humble and obedient to God, and that her love for Christ is
overpowering her other responses. Heliseus goes to Juliana's
father, Affricanus, and complains of the insults that she has

heaped on him. Juliana's father also becomes angry, and swears that he will not spare his daughter if Heliseus's complaint proves true.

He tries persuasion:

> You are my daughter, the dearest
> and the sweetest in my heart,
> the only light of my eyes on earth.
> Juliana, through your hostility
> you have taken this course foolishly
>   and unnecessarily
> and against the judgement of the wise.
> You reject your bridegroom too decidedly
> consulting only yourself; he is of higher status
>   than you,
> more noble in the world's view, richer
> in possessions and wealth. He is a valuable friend.
> So it is proper that you do not set aside completely
> this man's love and his lasting affection.

Once again, respect for parents and elders, loving counsel and cool wisdom are set aside. But these things are shown to be superficial and deceptive in the event. At any rate, Juliana resists Affricanus's blandishments. So he tries threats. They do not work either.

> Then the father was maddened with rage and
>   savage,
> fierce and grim in heart against his daughter.
> He commanded her to be scourged, chastised with
>   torture,
> afflicted with torments, and said these words:
> 'Change your mind, and turn aside from the words

which you foolishly spoke earlier
when you refused to sacrifice to our gods.'
Juliana, undaunted in her thought,
answered him:
'You will never teach me to render tribute
to deceitful, deaf and dumb
idols, enemies of the soul,
the worst servants of torment.
For I worship the Prince of glory,
Prince of the world and of all majesty,
and him alone I trust completely,
that he will be my protector,
my helper and my Saviour against hellish foes.'

Juliana is led to the public judgement before Heliseus. He,
too, tries flattery and threat.

'My sweetest Juliana,
light of the sun! You are radiant,
possessed of boundless grace, and the beauty of
      youth.
If you will yet sacrifice to our gods,
and look to them for merciful protection,
grace from the holy gods, you will be saved from
numberless torments, horrible evils,
cruelly performed, which are prepared for you
if you refuse to offer true sacrifices.'
The noble girl replied,
'You will never bring about what your boasts
      threaten,
nor will you prepare so many fierce torments
that I will love your friendship,
unless you abandon the deceits

> of heathen sacrifice, and wisely acknowledge
> the God of glory, the Creator of spirits,
> the Lord of humanity, to whom belongs power
> over all created things for ever and ever.'

The threatening tone of Heliseus's speech is chilling and this undermines the validity of his praise for her and the argument that Juliana should relent. But Cynewulf tries to make him sound convincing: looking to the gods – 'our gods' – for protection and making true sacrifices were no doubt things that were said by heathens in Anglo-Saxon times as well as earlier, and might have had a familiar ring to some in Cynewulf's audience. But Juliana is in no doubt: she worships the one true God, and all others are idols. She does not simply refuse Heliseus, however. All can be resolved if he becomes a Christian. Heliseus becomes angry at this, and adds colour to his threats of torture. Juliana replies that she fears nothing. So the suffering starts.

TORTURE

In his fury, Heliseus orders Juliana to be taken away and put to various tortures.

> It seemed an unworthy thing to the leader of
>   the people
> that he was unable to change the mind
> and determination of the virgin. He ordered her
>   to be
> hung up by the hair, tied up in a high tree,
> where the girl bright as the sun endured beating,
> endlessly fierce attack, for six hours a day.
> And then the hated foe had her forthwith

taken down again, and ordered her to be taken
to prison. Love of Christ
was firmly enclosed within the confines of her heart,
the strength of her gentle spirit was unbroken.

Heliseus is humiliated by Juliana's resistance. Cynewulf gently
reminds us that it is love for Christ that motivates her, and
that she has not become unfeminine. She is still gentle and
committed to her love. Even the torture of being tied up in a
tree by her hair and beaten, only makes more evident her
beauty: she is lifted up and shines in the sky like the sun.

DIALOGUE WITH A DEMON

In the prison, she is tempted to give in by the devil disguised
as an angel. In her confusion she calls out to God, and a sweet
voice tells her to grab the devil and force him to tell her who
he is and what he has done. He tells her how he instigated all
the evil things that led to Christ's death, and the persecution
that followed. She forces him further to admit his weakness
faced by any resolute Christian. And he also reveals how he
tempts people and lures them to destruction. When finally
Juliana is led out of the prison, she drags him along, before
abruptly letting him depart with his tail between his legs.

The interview with the devil is the longest part of the
poem as it stands in the manuscript. It takes the theme of
deception, which has been practised by Affricanus and
Heliseus already, and shows how Christians can resist it,
through love of Christ and knowledge of Christian teaching.
C.S. Lewis was not the first to make devils teach Christians.
This is the most obviously didactic part of the poem, and it
also has a robust kind of humour, as the devil is humiliated
and cowed by the young woman.

TORTURE AGAIN

A missing leaf in the manuscript makes it difficult to know
what comes before the next passage, except that Juliana has
been put to torture in fire.

> Then the angel of God came
> shining in his trappings, scattered the fire
> and freed and protected the guiltless
> and sinless girl; he dispersed the fiercely raging
> fire in the middle of which stood the holy one,
> foremost of women, safe and sound.
> That was a difficult thing for the wealthy man
>   Heliseus to put up with,
> when, in the presence of everyone, he could do
>   nothing to change it.
> The sin-stained man then cast about for a way to
> bring about her death with the greatest pain
> and the severest torments. The devil was not slow
>   to help.
> He advised him; and Heliseus had made, with
>   great skill and savage outcries,
> an earthen vessel; and he had it set around
>   with branches
> of trees from the forest. Then the severe
>   man ordered
> that the vessel be filled with lead,
> and then he had them light the greatest pyre,
> kindle the fire. It was surrounded with flames
> on every side, and the bath of lead boiled in the
>   heat.
> Then the man swollen with rage quickly ordered
> the sinless girl without guilt

to be thrust into the boiling lead. Then the fire
   was scattered
and the flame burned aimlessly; the lead
   went everywhere,
fiercely hot. Warriors were seized
with terror because of its flow. In total, 75 men
of the heathen army were burnt
through the blast of the fire. But the holy woman
   stood there
with untouched beauty: neither hem nor dress,
neither hair nor skin, neither body nor limbs,
were damaged by the fire. She stood in the flames
completely safe. She gave thanks for all
   these things
to the Lord of lords.

Heliseus has been thwarted in so many ways, he is at the limit
of his imagination. But Cynewulf is in control of his material.
He shows us the feverish preparations and the thoroughness
of the job done. But the expectation of the men is turned
on its head: the calm girl looks on untouched as those who
were brave as they put her into the pot of lead are seized with
terror when the lead spurts out. The stark statement that 75
died in the accident tells us the scale of Heliseus's mad rage.
But like Shadrach, Meshach and Abednego who survived
Nebuchadnezzar's fiery furnace, Juliana is unscathed and not
even the smell of fire clings to her.

DEATH

Finally, utterly maddened by these things, Heliseus orders
Juliana to be beheaded. The devil whom she earlier humiliated leads the procession, but is dismissed by a single glance

from the heroine. After an earnest exhortation to the people, Juliana is put to death by beheading. She becomes 'one of those who had been beheaded because of their testimony for Jesus and because of the word of God' as the book of Revelation refers to martyrs (20:4). Heliseus becomes frightened and flees by ship, and the ship goes down with all hands. But Juliana's body is laid to rest with praise to God. And Cynewulf closes by asking that the martyr might help him as he contemplates his own death.

ORDINARINESS

Cynewulf's *Juliana* is an attractive, dramatic poem. The story does not dwell at uncomfortable length on the tortures she suffers, but gives more space to the teaching material going under the disguise of the confession forced out of the devil. Juliana's own speeches, often echoing the Bible, also urge people to convert to Christianity, and her example reinforces the lesson that purity is preferable to comfort. So the martyrdom serves a purpose in Christian teaching. But it also taps into ordinary, everyday conflicts and feelings. In her forthrightness, Juliana becomes a recognizable, if not completely believable, teenage girl; and the anger of both her father and her suitor, while it takes extreme forms, is nevertheless an emotion felt by many older people in their relationships with younger people. While at one level the poem works as a kind of sermon, at another it explores human emotions within the framework of a conventional story.

ST ALBAN

Bede told the story of another martyr, closer to home, in his *Ecclesiastical History*. St Alban was one of the British

Christians martyred under the emperor Diocletian. He was widely famed and honoured throughout England, and the Scandinavians borrowed the cult and spread it in their lands. The story is told here by Ælfric, in his Old English version from *The Lives of the Saints*.

A certain heathen emperor called Diocletian was chosen as Caesar over all the world, though he was bloodthirsty, 286 years after Christ's birth. A savage persecutor, he reigned 20 years, and killed, and ordered to be killed, all the Christians that he could find, and burned down churches, and robbed the innocent. And this wicked persecution spread across the entire world for a whole decade until it came eventually to England, and there it killed many who believed in Christ.

One of these was the noble martyr Alban, who was also killed in this persecution for faith in Christ, as we shall make known here. In those days the bloodthirsty persecution came to England from the wicked emperor, and the executioners seized Christians everywhere with excessive madness. Then a priest escaped from them. He ran secretly to Alban's house and there lay hidden from his hateful persecutors. And Alban took him in, though he was not baptized. Then the priest, as he loved God, began to sing his offices, and fast severely, and praise his Lord day and night, and in the meantime to teach the true faith to the noble Alban, until he believed in the true God and turned away from heathenism and became truly a Christian and very devout.

The priest then lived with the noble man until the ealdorman who persecuted the Christians discovered that he was there. And, full of anger, he quickly commanded him to be brought before him. Then the messengers came to Alban's house, but Alban went out to the persecutors with the priest's cloak on as if he were the priest; and he had no intention of betraying him to the wicked persecutors. He was then bound and immediately brought to the wicked judge who was making devilish sacrifices to his gods with his associates. As soon as he looked upon the righteous martyr, the judge became fiendishly savage, because Alban had received the fleeing priest, and had given himself up to be killed in his place. He commanded him to be led to make the heathen sacrifices, and said that he himself must receive the severe torment he, the judge, had intended for the priest, if he had been able to catch him, unless he quickly submitted to his abominable gods. But Alban was not afraid of his devilish threats, because he was supported by God's weapons in the spiritual battle, and said that he had no intention of obeying the judge's commands, nor of submitting to heathen sacrifices.

Then the judge quickly asked, saying 'Of what tribe are you, or of what family?' Then Alban answered the wicked man thus: 'What concern is it of yours what my tribe might be? But if you wish to hear the truth I will tell you quickly that I am a Christian and will always worship Christ.' The judge said to him, 'Tell me your name without delay, now I ask you thus.' God's champion said to the murderer thus: 'My name is Alban, and I believe in the Saviour who is true God, and made all created things; I pray to him, and will always

worship him.' The murderer answered the faithful
man: 'If you wish to have the joy of this eternal
life, then you must not delay offering to the glorious gods with great humility.' Alban answered him,
'Your offerings to the gods, which you offer to
devils, cannot help you, nor bring about your
desires. But you will receive as your reward eternal
torments in spacious hell.'

Then the judge became fiendishly enraged and
commanded the holy martyr to be scourged. He
thought that he would be able, by means of the
scourging, to wear down his mental steadfastness,
and then compel him to do what he wanted. But
the blessed martyr was strengthened by God, and
very patiently bore this scourging, and with cheerful courage thanked God for it. Then the judge saw
that he would not be able to overcome the holy
man by means of those hateful torments, nor make
him turn from Christ, and he commanded him to
be killed by beheading for the Saviour's name.

The heathen men then did as they were commanded by the judge, and led the holy man away
to be beheaded, but they were hindered for a long
time at a bridge. And they stood there until the
evening because of the huge crowd of men and
women, who had been aroused and had come to
the martyr, and went with him. It then happened
that the unbelieving judge sat without food in the
town until evening, without being served at all,
unwillingly fasting.

So then Alban wanted to hurry to death, and
went to the river when he could not pass over the
bridge. And he looked up to heaven praying to the

Saviour, and the river immediately dried up before him, and a way was made across just as he had desired from God. Then the executioner whose duty it was to kill him was aroused by that miracle and threw away his sword and ran quickly when they got across the river, and fell at his feet full of faith. He wanted to die with Alban rather than kill him. He was then united by resolute faith with the holy man whom he was responsible for beheading, and the sword lay there shining before them, and not one of them had any wish to kill him.

There was near to the holy man a pleasant, and also a very smooth, hill decorated with plants in full beauty. Then Alban went quickly there, and immediately asked God to give him water upon that hill, and he did so. Then a stream ran there at Alban's feet, so that people might recognize his power with God, when the stream ran down from the steep hill. He was then beheaded for the sake of the Saviour's name on the hill, and departed to his Lord with victorious martyrdom and with true faith. But his slayer was not allowed to remain healthy, because both of his eyes burst out of him and fell to the earth with Alban's head, so that he could recognize whom he had killed. Afterwards they beheaded the faithful warrior who did not wish to behead the holy man, and he lay with Alban believing in God, and baptized with his blood, and departed to heaven.

When the executioners went back to their lord, and told him the wonderful signs that Alban had done, and how the man who had beheaded him had become blind, then he commanded the persecution to be given up and spoke honourably about the holy martyrs whom he was not able to turn from God's faith by means of terrible tortures. In the same persecution Aaron and Julius and many other men and women, far and wide throughout England, were killed for the faith of Christ, oppressed by tortures, and they departed victorious to the true life.

Then the persecution came to an end and the Christians came out of the woods and the wastelands where they had been hidden. And they went among the people and restored Christianity, and rebuilt the churches that had been destroyed, and lived in peace with true faith. They also built a noble church for the holy Alban where he was buried, and often miracles were performed there, to the praise of the Saviour who lives forever in eternity.

This happened before the conflict came through Hengist and Horsa, who defeated the Britons. After that, Christianity was again dishonoured until Augustine re-established it according to the teaching of Gregory the faithful pope.

Glory and praise be to the beneficent Creator, who saved our fathers from their enemies and converted them to baptism by means of his preachers. Amen.

SIMILARITIES AND DIFFERENCES

There is a large measure of similarity between this and the story of St Juliana. The persecutors are madly irrational, savage, and driven by the devil. The saint is calm, rational, unafraid. There is the same debate about the relative merits of the gods and God. The persecutors try to force the saint to sacrifice to the false gods, a historically documented test recorded in the letters of Pliny to the Emperor Trajan early in the second century. The saint resists, with the assertion that the gods are devils or idols, a reference from the Bible (Psalm 96:5, 1 Chronicles 16:26). There is beating and beheading for the martyr and the same prompt retribution for the perpetrator of the martyrdom.

But these similarities notwithstanding, there are also differences. The grim humour here comes from the poetic justice on the executioner who lost his eyes 'so that he could recognize whom he had killed' – the play on seeing and recognizing is Ælfric's addition to Bede. Moreover, in this story there is an instant 'model' response from the designated executioner, who dies with Alban, and from the judge who immediately suspends the persecution when he hears about how Alban died. These suggest the way the audience of the homily should respond, with eager enquiry and active faith. But perhaps one of the most interesting ways that the story differs from *Juliana* and indeed from Bede, is the way that Ælfric goes as far as in conscience he can towards making Alban English. Three times he tells us that these events took place in England, though at the end he gives a rather vague note to the effect that this was before Hengist and Horsa invaded. It was essential in Bede's story that his audience understood that Alban was British. But Ælfric wanted the support of the martyrs in the national crisis that confronted England, namely the Viking attacks, so he was prepared to borrow one.

ST EDMUND, KING AND MARTYR

An English martyr Ælfric did not have to borrow was provided by the Viking army which roved around the country
from 865 onwards. This army took over large tracts of terri-
tory and sent King Alfred of Wessex into hiding. One of the
kings defeated in the process was King Edmund of East
Anglia. Not much is known about him, and the earliest
sources seem to indicate that he died in battle. But quite soon
after his death, a cult grew up, and it was given credibility by
the writing of a Latin martyrdom by the Frankish scholar,
Abbo of Fleury, when he visited England in the years 985–7.
Abbo's story is long and detailed, and in it Edmund is a complete paragon. Ælfric cut the story down considerably when
he included it in his *Lives of the Saints* homilies a few years
later. This is the martyrdom part of Ælfric's version.

> King Edmund of the East Angles, the blessed, was
> wise and honourable, and constantly honoured
> almighty God by his life of noble virtue. He was
> humble and good and so singlemindedly constant
> that he never wished to stoop to shameful vices,
> nor did he ever deviate from his virtuous ways. But
> he always remembered the true teaching, 'If you
> are a leader of men, do not raise yourself up, but be
> among men as one of them.' He was liberal to the
> poor and widows like a father, and always guided
> his people with benevolence into ways of good-
> ness, and restrained the violent, and lived happily
> in the true faith.
>
> In due course it happened that the Danish
> people with a fleet travelled far and wide through
> the land, harrying and killing, as is their habit. The

most important leaders of the sailors were Hinguar and Hubba, united through the devil. They landed with their ships in Northumbria, and laid waste the land and killed the people. Then, having won victory through savagery, Hinguar turned east with his ships, and left Hubba in Northumbria. Hinguar arrived by rowing among the East Anglians in the year that Prince Alfred, who later became famous as the king of the West Saxons, was 21. And the aforementioned Hinguar suddenly crept like a wolf upon the land, and struck the people, men, women and innocent children, and shamefully oppressed the innocent Christians.

Soon after that, he sent a vaunting message to King Edmund, demanding that he should offer his allegiance to Hinguar if he valued his life. The messenger then approached King Edmund and quickly gave him Hinguar's message, 'Hinguar our king, who is brave and victorious by land and sea, has power over many nations, and has come now with his army suddenly upon this land, so that he may make his winter base here with his army. Now he commands you to share your secret treasures and your ancestral valuables quickly with him, and be his tributary king if you want to live. For you do not have the power to be able to resist him.'

At this, King Edmund called a bishop who was conveniently near and discussed with him how he should reply to the savage Hinguar. The bishop was struck with fear because of the sudden turn of events and the threat to the king's life, and said that it seemed to him the best thing if the king were to submit to Hinguar's demands. The king kept silent and looked at the earth, and then said to the bishop in regal manner, 'Bishop, the wretched inhabitants of this land are shamefully mistreated, and I would now rather die in battle if my people might be allowed to enjoy their land.' The bishop said, 'O dear king, your people lie slain and you do not have the resources to be able to fight; and these sailors will come and capture you alive unless you save your life by means of flight, or by submitting to them protect yourself.' Then Edmund, full of courage as he was, said, 'This is what I ask for and the desire of my heart: that I do not survive after my beloved thanes with their children and wives have been suddenly slain in their beds by these sailors. It was never my way to take to flight, but I wished rather to die, if I had to, for the sake of my own land. Almighty God knows that I have no intention of ever turning aside from worship of him, or away from his true love whether I live or die.'

After these words, Edmund turned to the messenger that Hinguar had sent to him, and boldly said, 'Truly you deserve death now, but I do not wish to sully my clean hands with your filthy blood. For I follow Christ who gave us an example in this. I will gladly be slain by you if that is what God ordains. Go now, with all speed, and tell your cruel lord, "Never will Edmund, alive, submit to Hinguar the savage general, unless he, Hinguar, first submits in faith to the Saviour Christ in this land."'

The messenger went quickly away, and on the road he met the savage Hinguar hurrying towards Edmund with all his army. And he told the wicked man how he was answered. Hinguar then arrogantly commanded his Vikings to look out especially for the king who had rejected his offer, and immediately bind him.

So King Edmund stood in his hall when Hinguar came, and mindful of the Saviour, threw down his weapons. He wished to follow Christ's example, who forbade Peter to fight with weapons against the savage Jews. So the wicked men bound Edmund and abused him insultingly, and beat him with rods, and afterwards took the faithful king to a firmly rooted tree, and tied him to it with strong ropes, and then scourged him for a long time with whips. Between strokes, he kept calling out in true faith to the Saviour Christ. Because of his faith, and because he kept calling for help to Christ, the heathens became madly enraged. They shot at him, for their amusement, until he was covered with their missiles like the bristles on a hedgehog, just as St Sebastian was. Hinguar the wicked sailor saw that the noble king had no intention of renouncing Christ, but kept calling out to him with resolute faith. So he ordered him to be beheaded, and the heathen did it. Even while he was still calling upon Christ, the heathen led away the holy man to his death, and with a single blow cut off his head, and his happy soul passed to Christ. A certain man was there nearby, kept hidden from the heathen by God, who heard all this and told it afterwards just as we have related it here.

With some variations, the things that happen to Edmund are those that happened to Juliana and Alban. The Viking

messenger threatens, and the English bishop reasons, just as
Heliseus and Affricanus did with Juliana. But like both
Juliana and Alban, Edmund desires martyrdom rather than
the ignominious alternative laid before him. Like Juliana,
Edmund promises to submit to Hinguar, if Hinguar first
becomes a Christian. The men opposed to Edmund are both
savage and demonic, and as usual, become madly enraged by
the faith and resistance of the martyr. Making no headway in
breaking Edmund down with beatings and shooting him full
of arrows, the Vikings give him the crown of martyrdom by
beheading. And just as *Juliana* dealt with real human emotions under cover of the conventional story, so also this story
raises questions about how England might be defended, how
Christians ought to react to oppression, and whether they
ought to fight at all. There is humour later, as Edmund's
hidden head calls out to people looking for it. In short, whatever the factual truth of the story, it does very well all the
things that martyrdom stories are intended to do.

   There was evidently a popular cult of St Edmund, particularly among the descendants of the Viking settlers in the
Danelaw, and this spread to Scandinavia. Once again Ælfric
was making sure that the English martyr was seen to be on
the side of the English, and he makes this clear at the end of
the homily:

> the English nation is not deprived of the Lord's
> saints since in England there lie such saints as this
> holy king [Edmund], the blessed Cuthbert, St
> Æthelthryth of Ely and her sister incorrupt in
> body, for the confirmation of the faith. There are
> also many other saints among the English who
> work many miracles, as is widely known, to the
> praise of the Almighty in whom they believed.

For Ælfric and others, stories of the saints and martyrs played a political as well as a spiritual role in Anglo-Saxon England.

ST EDWARD, KING AND MARTYR

This point is made clearer by the existence of a popular cult of St Edward. Edward was king 975–8, and half-brother of King Æthelred the Unready. Edward was killed in 978, on the order of his mother, it was widely believed. His death was covered up, and Archbishop Wulfstan believed that his body had been burnt because he says so in his famous *Sermo Lupi* of 1014. The *Anglo-Saxon Chronicle* commemorates Edward in verse, but does not give much away about the forensic details, who did it, when, where, why and how.

> No worse deed was done by English people than this
> since they first came to the land of Britain.
> Men murdered him, but God made him great.
> He was in life an earthly king,
> now after death he is a heavenly saint;
> his earthly kinsmen had no desire to avenge him,
> but his heavenly Father has greatly avenged him;
> the earthly slayers wished to hide his memory in
>   the earth,
> but the heavenly Avenger has spread his memory
>   in heaven and on earth.
> Those who had no desire to bow to his living body
> now humbly bend on their knees to his
>   dead bones.
> Now we can perceive that human wisdom
>   and contrivances
> and counsels are of no value against God's plan.

This version of the *Anglo-Saxon Chronicle* was written by someone deeply disillusioned with Æthelred's reign, which ultimately saw the English capitulate to Cnut and his Vikings. But even this writer seems guarded in what he says; the cover-up was still effective some years after the killing. When he became king, Cnut saw that it might be to his advantage to make the cult official, and did so, and we might guess that rumours to the disadvantage of his predecessor circulated with his encouragement. At the end of the 11th century, a martyr-dom was written, and it exists in several manuscripts and is excerpted and borrowed by many writers. This is the short-ened version of the story from William of Malmesbury's *History of the English Kings.*

> In the year of the Lord's incarnation 975, Edward, the son of Edgar, began to reign and he held the throne three and a half years. Dunstan, with the agreement of the other bishops, raised him to the royal dignity, against the will of some of the nobility, and of his stepmother, so it is said, who wanted to advance her son Æthelred, a child of barely seven years old, so that she herself could reign in his name. From then on, evil increased among the people, and the happiness of the realm decreased. At that time a comet was seen, which, we are reliably informed, portends either plague in the land or a change of rule. A failure of the crops soon followed, bringing famine to the people, and death to cattle...
>
> King Edward treated his young brother and step-mother warmly, having only the name of king for himself, but allowing them all other things. He fol-lowed in the footsteps of his father's piety, listening

to good counsel and taking it to heart. But the woman, with the hatred of a stepmother and the cunning of a serpent, began to think of a plot against her stepson's life so that not even the name of king should be lacking to her son. She carried it out as follows. He was coming home, tired from hunting, breathless and thirsty from the exercise; his companions were following the dogs wherever chance led them; and having heard that they were to stay in a nearby village, the young man alone, in his innocence suspecting nothing and judging others indeed as he judged himself, urged his horse there at full speed.

On his arrival, his stepmother with a woman's charm drew his attention to herself, and after a kiss, offered him a drink. While he was eagerly drinking it, she had him stabbed with a dagger by one of her servants. Having been badly wounded, with what strength remained to him he urged his horse on so as to join the others. But one foot slipped, and he was dragged through remote tracks by the other, leaving streams of blood as clear evidence of his death to those who looked for him.

Then they ordered him to be buried without honour at Wareham, grudging him indeed consecrated ground when dead, just as they had grudged him the royal title when he was alive. So they enjoyed public and festive rejoicing, as if they had buried his memory when they buried his body. But divine grace acknowledged him, and honoured the innocent victim with the glory of miracles: so much are human judgements outweighed by heavenly ones. Lights shone from the sky there, a lame man walked there, a dumb man regained speech there, and there every kind of illness gave place to health. Word of this spread throughout England and made the martyr's merits famous.

There are a number of distinct echoes of the *Chronicle*'s verse here, particularly as divine grace confounds the plans of the conspirators. Perhaps the most remarkable thing we find, though, is that Edward has become a martyr, with all the trappings and miracles of the martyrs' cults, but without any of the usual features of martyrdom as it had come down to the Anglo-Saxons. Edward, though a kind man in the story, was not even known as an outstanding Christian; he was not killed for his faith; he was not beaten or beheaded; there is little in the story to teach Christian truth, or encourage Christian action.

POPULAR AND POLITICAL

In short, Edward was apparently the victim of political assassination: it was the popular reaction against that dastardly action that transformed him into a martyr. Moreover, the growth of the cult took place under predominantly non-English kings, from Cnut to William the Conqueror and his sons. If it was initially given encouragement by Cnut, the cult became part of an English reaction to the Normans. It gave the oppressed English a sense that God was on their side. Edward became a symbol, someone who was an innocent victim of political forces. In the English imagination of the time, he became someone not unlike Diana, Princess of Wales in our own time.

ST ÆLFHEAH

Edward became a martyr despite the unlikeness of his death to the approved martyrdoms of the Roman tradition. Popular veneration was crucial. Archbishop Ælfheah became a martyr despite a rather close investigation into the circumstances of his death by the Norman church hierarchy. The *Anglo-Saxon Chronicle* records the events under the annals for the years 1011 and 1012.

> In this year between the Festival of the Nativity of St Mary and Michaelmas, the Viking army surrounded Canterbury. They got into it by treachery, because Ælfmær, whose life Archbishop Ælfheah had saved, betrayed it to them. There they seized the Archbishop Ælfheah and Ælfweard the king's reeve and Leofwine the abbot and Godwine the bishop. They allowed abbot Ælfmær to go free. In the city they seized all those in holy orders, men and women, and it is impossible for anyone to say how great a part of the people it was. They stayed in the town after that as long as they wished to, and when they had searched all through it they returned to the ships, and led the archbishop captive with them:

> He who formerly was the head of the English
> and of Christendom was then a captive.
> There might then be seen wretchedness
> where before bliss was seen
> in the wretched town whence to us first came
> Christianity and prosperity before God and in the
>   world.

And they had the archbishop in their power up until the time when they martyred him.

On the Saturday before the Easter of the year 1012, the Viking army became enraged against the bishop, because he did not wish them to be given any money and forbade that anything should be given in ransom for him. They were also very drunk, because wine from the south had been brought there. They took the bishop and led him to their meeting on the Saturday evening of Easter week, and there pelted him to death with bones and with skulls of cattle. One of them struck him with an iron axe on the head, so that he fell down from the stroke, and his holy blood fell on to the earth. His holy soul he sent forth to God's kingdom.

Bishops Eadnoth and Ælfhun and the citizens of Canterbury received his holy body in the morning and carried it to London with all honour, and buried him in St Paul's minster. And now God reveals the holy martyr's powers there.

With the martyrdom of Ælfheah, we return to sober history. The objection to Ælfheah as a martyr arose in a discussion between Anselm and Lanfranc the Norman archbishop of Canterbury in the second half of the 11th century; and it was that he did not explicitly die for his faith. But many of the other features of martyrdoms are here: persecution of Christians, savage and enraged enemies, the chance of escape not taken. In addition there are individualizing details of treachery and humiliation and mode of death. The writer of the *Chronicle* had no doubt that this was a martyrdom, and the similarity between the brief details of the martyrdom given in the last two paragraphs quoted above and typical entries in the various martyrologies is striking.

As a result of the discussion between Anselm and Lanfranc, an official Latin martyrdom was written by a man called Osbern, but it strives too hard to fit Ælfheah into the classical martyr mould, with the result that it is less believable than the shocking account of the *Chronicle*. Osbern takes away the animal bones and skulls, and replaces them with stones so that Ælfheah is more like St Stephen. Ælfheah is also fitted with all becoming Christian virtues, and Osbern, sensitive to the issue of whether Ælfheah died for his faith, also makes much of his attempts to convert his captors and fellow prisoners.

MARTYRS AND MEANING

Martyrdoms happened in history. There are many more martyrdom stories from Anglo-Saxon England that it has been possible to mention here. The stories circulated among the people and became elaborated, and were used, or became popular, for many different reasons. Bede saw St Alban as a beacon of hope for the British, but Ælfric borrowed him for the English. Cynewulf used the story of St Juliana for teaching about the devil's deceptions and for personal comfort. Ælfric made that comfort and encouragement more general by showing the heroism and faith of English St Edmund against the Vikings. The ordinary people seem to have taken St Edward to their hearts for little other reason than that he was the victim of political scheming and was also vindicated by God. And Ælfheah was certainly murdered in a shocking fashion to become another martyr of the Vikings, though Osbern did not quite like the way in which it happened.

Martyr stories were important to the Anglo-Saxons. The martyrs gave meaning to what would in purely human terms be meaningless cruelty and oppression. They showed it was possible to resist evil and temptation, even to the extent of shedding their blood. Through their heavenly powers they were able to help and give courage to suffering people. They helped sustain the Christian understanding of the world as a passing, difficult phase of preparation for heaven, and one in which it was worth suffering for the sake of the joy to come. They also showed how earthly faith and courage gave spiritual power which was not lost, but augmented, after their death. Though the martyrs make light of dying, and it might seem that they undervalue life in their desire for martyrdom, the stories are essentially life-affirming. The martyrs face the facts of hatred and oppression and deceit and contempt, and assert an alternative of love and faith and courage. They follow in the footsteps of Christ.

A Latin prayer for the feast of St Edmund

20 November: the birth of St Edmund

Ineffable and merciful God, who gave the most
blessed King Edmund to overcome his enemies in
dying for your name, graciously grant to your servants by his help that they may destroy in
themselves the temptations of the ancient enemy
and conquer through Jesus Christ our Lord.
Alleluia.

The 'birth' in the title is the day of St Edmund's martyrdom,
the day he was born to eternal life, and overcame his enemies
through death. So the martyr turns on their head the conventions of the world, conventions to which the secular Anglo-
Saxons were deeply attached. The prayer was apparently
composed before the death of King Æthelred, when the
prospect of the Anglo-Saxons conquering their Viking enemies looked very remote, and it offers a hope of spiritual
victory to the long-suffering English.

ÆLFRIC AND WULFSTAN

 The needs of the Church change according to the circumstances in which it lives. Bede was a great teacher in the eighth century, but the settled kind of life which allowed him to flourish was simply not possible for other great teachers, such as Ælfric and Wulfstan in the 10th and 11th centuries. Ælfric and Wulfstan had to adapt to the conditions that life presented them with, and they did it well. But they did not both do it in the same way. They demonstrate in their lives and works a fact which is sometimes lost sight of in the modern world: that different people contribute in their own distinctive way to the vitality of the Church.

Ælfric and Wulfstan lived in perilous times. Both came to prominence in the reign of Æthelred the Unready, 978–1016, at the time of renewed Viking attacks on England. Both wrote extensively, particularly in the form of homilies or sermons, but in many other forms too. Both were learned men, well-educated in the scriptures and in Christian authors. The works of both were copied and used by later writers, when much of Old English literature was discarded and some manuscripts were cut up to provide binding for later works. The two corresponded with each other and knew each other's work. Wulfstan in particular used Ælfric's work in his own compositions. Yet no one who has read the two could reasonably confuse them. Each has his own very distinctive style and preoccupations.

ÆLFRIC

Ælfric was educated at Winchester under the great bishop Æthelwold, one of the leaders in the reformation of Benedictine monasticism in the 10th century. Ælfric recorded his debt to Æthelwold when he composed his *Life* of Æthelwold in Latin, an abbreviation of an earlier work by another man. Although Ælfric used this other work, he writes in the preface that he has done it 'in a brief narrative after my own fashion, even though it is rough: I have written down what I have learned from you [Bishop Cenwulf and the monks of Winchester] or other reliable witnesses, so that it will not be given over to oblivion because of the dearth of writers'.

Written sometime around 1005–6, this is among Ælfric's latest datable works. As well as recording his personal debt to a great saint and teacher, and his affection for his old school of Winchester, this brief prologue to the *Life* outlines Ælfric's lifelong concerns. He wishes above all to make information available to those who do not have it, and who might otherwise never have it; he wishes to make information accessible, by writing it in his own style, which is clear and simple (what he calls rough or rustic); and he wishes to pass on the fruit of his researches as accurately as he can.

Ælfric was born around the middle of the 10th century, though it is not certain precisely when or where. In his preface to his translation of Genesis, he remarks that he had as teacher a priest who taught him the facts of the biblical story without interpretation or moral warning. This made Ælfric very chary about translating the Old Testament books, because the unadorned text might lead astray the ignorant. And, moreover, it helped form his desire to educate people by his writing.

> Once I knew a certain priest, who was my school-master at the time, and he had the book of Genesis, and knew a certain amount of Latin. He said of the patriarch Jacob that he had four wives – two sisters and their two maidservants. It was true what he said, but he did not know, nor I either at that point, how great is the division between the old law and the new. In the beginning of the world, brother had sister as wife, and sometimes even father bred with his own daughter, and many had more than one wife for the increase of the popula-tion, and in the early days people could only marry their own close family. If anyone wishes to live in this fashion now, since the coming of Christ, as people lived then before or under the law of Moses, that person is no Christian, and he does not deserve to have any Christian eat with him.

ABBOT ÆLFRIC

During his schooling and later work at Winchester under St Æthelwold, Ælfric seems to have come to the notice of Æthelweard, a learned lay nobleman who translated a version of the *Anglo-Saxon Chronicle* into Latin. It was Æthelweard who commissioned the translation of Genesis, and it was Æthelweard's son, Æthelmær, who encouraged Ælfric to move to the newly founded (or refounded) monastery at Cerne Abbas in Dorset, where Ælfric wrote most of his homilies.

Later Æthelmær chose Ælfric as abbot for the monastery the nobleman founded at Eynsham near Oxford, and Ælfric was there by 1006.

Æthelmær is mentioned with affection and respect in the preface to Ælfric's *Catholic Homilies*. These are two sets of sermons mostly on the gospel readings for the Sundays of the year, but also on the lives of saints. A later collection of homilies wholly devoted to accounts of the lives of the saints covers all the main saints in the English calendar. Ælfric's other major works, including a grammar and glossary for students of Latin, and his *Colloquy*, are mentioned elsewhere in this book. These works were most likely composed in response to the need of the monastery at Cerne for good teaching materials.

ÆLFRIC'S TEACHING

It is precisely those things that made him a good teacher that make his homilies and other works enjoyable and valuable. He constantly worries about his style. This is at least partly because he was educated by Æthelwold, whose Latin style is difficult and rather pompous; and partly perhaps because he avoids some of the more powerful effects of the oral English style of Archbishop Wulfstan. Ælfric achieves a smooth, rhythmical English which is, apart from elements of vocabulary, remarkably similar to modern English. He works hard to pass on the best information he has in accessible form, and he draws on a wide range of the best Christian authors, from the Bible, the church Fathers (Augustine, Jerome, Gregory and so on) through to the popular millennial writer Adso, a near-contemporary writing in France.

Here is Ælfric's preface to the *Catholic Homilies*. It seems to have been added to a revision of the original. And it functions

not only as a justification of the entire work in the light of
Ælfric's circumstances and the state of the world and education at the time, but also as a homily in its own right.

I, Ælfric, monk and mass-priest, despite the fact
that I am unequal to that role, was sent in the
days of King Æthelred from Bishop Ælfheah,
Æthelwold's successor, to a certain monastery
called Cerne by the request of Æthelmær the
thane, whose parentage and goodness are known
everywhere. Then it occurred to me – by the grace
of God I believe – that I should translate this book
from the Latin language into the English tongue,
not from confidence in great learning, but because
I saw and heard great heresy in many English
books, which ignorant people in their innocence
held to be great wisdom. And it grieved me that
they did not know and did not have the gospel
teachings among their writings, except only from
those people who know Latin and except from
those books that King Alfred wisely translated
from Latin into English, which are still available.
For this reason I presumed to begin this writing,
trusting in God, and also because people need good
doctrine especially at this time, which is the end of
the world. There will be many dangers among
humankind before the end comes, just as our Lord
says in the gospel to his disciples: 'Then there will
be such tribulations as never were from the beginning of the world. Many false Christs will come in
my name, saying, "I am Christ", and they will perform many signs and wonders to deceive humanity
and even the chosen ones if that were possible.

And if God did not cut short the days, all humankind would be destroyed; but for the sake of his chosen ones he will cut short the days.' Everyone will be able to withstand the coming temptation with God's help if he is encouraged by biblical teaching, because they who persevere in faith to the end will be preserved.

Many tribulations and miseries will come upon this earth before its end, and those things are the messengers of the eternal destruction of evil men, who, because of their crimes, will suffer forever in black hell. Then the Antichrist will come, who is a human being and true devil, just as our Saviour is truly human and God in a single person. And the visible devil will then do countless wonders, and claim that he himself is God, and he will intend to compel humanity to accept his heresy. But the time will not be long, because God's wrath will destroy him, and then the end of this world will come.

Christ our Lord healed the weak and the sick, and this devil that is called Antichrist (that is, translated, 'opposite-to-Christ') will weaken and make sick the healthy, and heal none from illness that he did not first injure. He and his followers will injure human bodies secretly through the devil's cunning, and will heal them publicly in the sight of all. But he will not be able to heal any that God himself made weak. With wickedness he will compel people to turn from faith in their Creator to his lies, who is the origin of all lies and wicked-ness. Almighty God will permit the wicked Antichrist to do signs and wonders and persecution for three and a half years, because in that time there will be so much evil and perversion among humanity that they will fully merit that devilish persecution: there will be eternal destruction for those who submit to him, and eternal joy for those who by faith resist him. God will permit his chosen thanes to be purified from all sins through those intense persecutions, just as gold is tested in the fire. Then the devil will slay all those that stand against him and they will then go to the kingdom of heaven by holy martyrdom. The devil will honour those who believe his lies, and they will have eternal torment as a reward for their error afterwards.

The wicked one, in the sight of all, will make fire come from above as if from heaven and as if he were God almighty, the One who has control of earth and heaven. But Christians must then remember what the devil did when he asked God if he could test Job. He made fire come from above as if from heaven, and burned all his sheep out in the field, together with the shepherds, except for the one who had to tell him about it. But the devil did not send fire from heaven then, though it came from above, because he himself was not in heaven after he was thrown out of there for his pride. And indeed the savage Antichrist does not have the power to send heavenly fire, though by the devil's cunning it might appear as such. Whoever knows this and under-stands his faith will be wiser, for it is possible that he might have to experience the great misery.

Our Lord commanded his disciples to instruct and teach all peoples those things that he himself

taught them. But there are now too few of those
who teach well and give a good example. The same
Lord cried out through his prophet Ezekiel, 'If you
do not oppose the unrighteous and warn him to
turn from his wickedness and live, then the wicked
will die in his unrighteousness and I will require his
blood (that is, his loss) from you. If you then warn
the wicked, and he does not wish to turn from his
wickedness, you will have saved your soul by that
warning, and the wicked will die in his unrighteousness.' Again, the Almighty said to the prophet
Isaiah, 'Cry out and do not cease, lift up your voice
like a trumpet, and tell my people their crimes, and
Jacob's family their sins.' Because of such commands it seemed to me that I would not be guiltless
with God if I did not desire to make known by
voice or through writings to other people the truth
of the gospel which he himself spoke and afterwards revealed to holy teachers.

I know very well that there are more learned
people on this earth than I am, but God reveals
his wonders through whoever he wishes. Like the
almighty Creator he is, he does his works through
his chosen ones, not because he needs our help,
but because we merit eternal life through the
accomplishment of his work. The Apostle Paul
said, 'We are God's helpers', but we can nevertheless do nothing for God without God's help.

Now I pray and implore in God's name that
if anyone wishes to copy this book he carefully
checks it against the original, in case through careless scribes we are led astray. He who writes lies
does great evil, such that he brings true doctrine

into false heresy, unless he corrects it. So whoever earlier corrupted things into error, must put them right if he wishes to be guiltless in God's judgement.

Ælfric followed in the footsteps of King Alfred in lamenting the fact that the populace were dependent for their Christian education on a declining number of individuals who knew Latin. There were a few books written in English still available, but they offered little help to the mass of people. Ordinary people simply had to accept what they heard because they could not read Latin and did not have access to the few English books there were, even if they could read English. Around this time there were increasing worries in the Church and secular hierarchy about the increase of heathenism and superstition. But few had the foresight or energy or power of King Alfred to tackle the issue head on by making provision for wider education and translating major books. The result was a downward spiral of error and ignorance.

Ælfric's remedy is elegantly simple and yet thorough. He identifies the problem, analyses its origins, and gives forthright but personally applied teaching to resolve it. The problem is ignorance and error. One source of this is the lack of readily available orthodox and authoritative teaching on the Christian faith, for reasons we have already noted. In supplying the defect, Ælfric makes it clear several times that he does not think of himself as a theological genius or an immensely learned man. Part of his argument is that good Christians are not necessarily of this kind. Rather, he talks of himself as an obedient man, willing to use his limited resources in the service of God. Moreover, his main purpose is, as he says, to make the gospel teachings available, simply and in English; and that is precisely what the *Catholic Homilies* do. The learning that Ælfric undoubtedly used in his writing is evident to the modern source-scholar, but would not have been evident to the people hearing the sermons, or indeed to most of the priests who used them.

THE END OF THE WORLD

Ælfric does what he can to address the problem of ignorance by composing the homilies. He moves seamlessly to another source of the problem. This is the deception of the devil and Antichrist at the end of the world. The body of the preface is teaching about the Last Days, in which Ælfric was convinced he was living. We have to deduce from Ælfric's teaching that there was speculation circulating about the end of the world and what it was, or would be, like. Certainly there was a conviction that the end of the first millennium would see the end of the world, and certainly there was sufficient persecution in the shape of Viking attacks going on at the time to fuel fears that this was the advent, or the prelude to the advent, of the Antichrist. But rather than reading the signs of the times from contemporary events, Ælfric is concerned to instruct people about the truth and show them how to discern the difference between devilish delusion and spiritual reality. He wants to equip people to persevere, and gives them the biblical knowledge to do it.

CARELESSNESS

A third source of the problem of error is mentioned at the end of the preface. All books were copied by hand and mistakes often crept in. A single careless stroke of the pen could completely change the meaning of a sentence. Modern scholars have names for countless kinds of omissions, repetitions, misspellings, inversions and variations. By way of an example of the vagaries of copying, in the 21 manuscript versions of the 42 or 43 words of Cædmon's *Hymn* in Old English not one is the same as another in spelling, or punctuation (which was minimal at this time anyway). Ælfric made this same plea for accuracy several times in his works. He is not pleading for mechanical accuracy here, as he might have been in his *Grammar*, but for fidelity to the source. Scribes were among those who had sufficient learning to have their own opinions, and as Ælfric has already indicated at the beginning of the preface, not all opinions are equally valid. His own enterprise of education could be undermined by faulty transmission of his teaching.

SERVICE

The impression of Ælfric we gain from the preface to the *Homilies* is of a man confident and clear in his own mind. A busy man, but one who senses the overriding priority of the need of the ordinary person. A man with a wide and sensitive grasp of biblical teaching, but unwilling to parade his knowledge. A humble and devout man who nevertheless does not pull his punches when it comes to teaching and warning people about error and its results. He does what he can, and by common consent of posterity, the *Catholic Homilies* and other works were among the most useful books produced at this time. But he knows that the enterprise of Christian education is one that involves a whole community: monks, teachers, preachers, scribes and people. He embraces them all, and calls them all to work with him in the service of God.

WULFSTAN

Wulfstan was a contemporary of Ælfric, but he moved in very different circles. He became bishop of London in 996 and archbishop of York in 1002 or 1003. He was buried and honoured at Ely, one of the most important monasteries and churches of the Danelaw, the northern and eastern parts of England controlled by the Danish settlers of King Alfred's day. As archbishop, he also held the see of Worcester until his death in 1023. He was not the first to do this, and the justification was that the northern church had been impoverished by the Viking attacks and settlements, and that Worcester could provide the revenue needed to support an archbishop. Some later historians blamed him severely. But whatever the justification, it is clear simply from the fact that the archbishop was in deep political water. Most of his ministry was among the Mercian and Northumbrian people who were to some extent marginalized politically and ecclesiastically by the West Saxon king Æthelred and the circumstances of the Viking wars going on at the time.

WULFSTAN'S WORKS

The list of Wulfstan's works is difficult to determine, since his style was imitated with varying degrees of success by many. But a good number of homilies, law codes, prose treatises and indeed poems can be attributed to him. The laws and treatises, such as *The Institutes of Polity* which is an outline of the duties of the various classes of people in Church and state, show Wulfstan's genius for systematic classification. If the law codes show Wulfstan's concern with just laws, the treatises show his concern with order in the widest possible sense, intellectual as well as social and political.

Wulfstan's laws, written for Kings Æthelred and Cnut, are quite different from the rather dry and curt statement of penalties that earlier laws consist of. They are mostly long, reasoned and detailed. They recognise the shades of grey in guilt, the variations in circumstances that make laws just or unjust in application, and they acknowledge the need to persuade people to obey the king and his laws. Social stability is the goal, and it is clear that Wulfstan knows what really goes on in the world. He makes connections between the abstract and the particular, the ideal and the real.

In the following homily, written around the time of his appointment to the archbishopric of York, we can see Wulfstan's ability to make the connections between what goes on in the world and the millennial ideas that were circulating at the time.

When his disciples asked our Lord about the end of the world, he said to them: When you see the abomination of desolation, etc. Woe to those who are pregnant and those nursing babies in those days. There will be troubles such as have never been since the beginning of the creation made by God until now, and such as never will be again, etc.

Dear people, our Lord's apostles asked him once about the end of this world. He then said to them that such miseries and such afflictions must come upon the world as had never before been and would never after happen again. And the gospel says: Woe to the women who then will be pregnant and at that dreadful time will be feeding their children. Look, it must needs get much worse in the world because of people's sins, for now is the time about which the Apostle Paul prophesied in the past. He said once to Bishop Timothy that in the last days of this world there would be dangerous times because of people's sins, and he said 'then men will love this false world all too greatly: they will be excessively grasping of worldly treasures, too many will be overly proud and all too insolent and too boastful; and some will become terribly disdainful of divine things and disapproving of doctrine and loving injustice; and some will become treacherous and suavely cunning and with bad faith guilty of sins'.

And let the one who experiences this know that now is the time that this world is disturbed with abundant crime and multifarious deceit, and that it is worse far and wide in the world, just as the gospel says: *Because of the increase of wickedness, the love of most will grow cold.* That is in English, because injustice grows all too widely, true love becomes cold. People do not love God as they should, human covenants do not count for anything, but injustice reigns far and wide and shaky covenants exist among people: and that is evident in many ways, let him who experiences it recognize it.

O! O! there was great joy then, and the best remedy among people, when Christ came into the world by human birth, and came as the greatest help and the best comfort to us all. And there is a great wickedness facing us now that Antichrist is to be born, let him who has to suffer it, endure it. Christ was the best of all children ever born; and Antichrist will be the worst of all children ever born into the world, past, present or future.

Now it must needs get much worse because his time is coming very close, just as it is written and was prophesied long ago: *After a thousand years Satan will be released.* That is in English, Satan will be freed after a thousand years. A thousand years and indeed more have now passed since Christ was among people in human form, and now Satan's bonds are much looser and Antichrist's time is very near, and so it is always the worse the longer it goes on in the world. People are faithless and the world is the worse for it – that hurts us all; and henceforth it will lie terribly heavy on the righteous poor and the innocent. Now the wicked and the deceitful increase so excessively in the world, and the greatest evil is correspondingly abroad among people: that is Antichrist himself, the arch-enemy.

O! Great was the persecution that Christians endured long ago in the world again and again, far and wide, through savage traitors; and indeed persecution must henceforth multiply, now the devil himself is allowed to wield his power and the children of the devil are allowed so greatly to terrify Christians. And while there was much persecution formerly, it was never like the persecution that is going to come after this. It was often the case formerly that God's saints worked many miracles publicly by the power of God among those who suffered the persecution, and by that means healed many a person. But it will not be like that at all in Antichrist's time. Saints will not be able to do any public miracles but must endure whatever is done to them. Then God himself will not reveal his powers nor miracles for a time as he often used to, but he will allow the devil Antichrist to rage and run riot, for a certain time, with those who support him.

He will be born as a man, but he will be completely filled with the spirit of the devil. And that visible fiend will do many amazing signs through the cunning of the devil, and through magic will multiply delusions. And for three and a half years he will reign over humankind and with his devilish cunning will deceive the greatest number of people who could ever be deceived by anything. And those that he cannot otherwise deceive with his wiles, he intends to threaten and terribly compel and dreadfully torture in many ways and force against their will so that they accept his falsehoods.

He will begin to lie in his devilish fashion and will deny Christ, and will claim that he himself is God's own son, and will reduce all too many to error. And God will permit him for a certain time to harm madly because of the things people have done, because people will be so ruined by their sins that the devil will then be allowed publicly to tempt them to see how many he can lure to eternal destruction. And those that are then so blessed that they continually and earnestly keep to God's truth and intend resolutely to persist in right belief – they must endure the greatest persecution that anyone ever endured in the world, greater even than happened anywhere in the past, or ever will come in the future. But the one who perseveres then will be blessed, for eternal comfort is ordained for him by God's power soon afterwards. Lo, is it any wonder that the human devil is allowed to harm the sinful severely, when God permits him to perform such a wonder on his own saints that Enoch and Elias were martyred by the arch-enemy? These two God had preserved in soul and body for the single purpose of protecting the people by their teaching, so that they would not all be utterly destroyed together by the devil who terrifies all people and afflicts the whole world.

There is no one alive who can say or conceive how evil it will be in that devilish time. Then a brother will not protect his brother, sometimes a father will not protect his child, nor a child his own father, nor relatives their kin, any more than strangers. And nations will fight and strive against each other before the time when this must happen. And there must rise up far and wide trouble and strife, slander and hatred and the plundering of robbers, battle and famine, burning and blood-letting and severe storms, plague and pestilence and many disasters. And many signs will be widely visible in the sun and moon and various stars, and many kinds of terror will happen on earth to frighten the people to the heart and to attack them with dread in many ways.

And it would all be destroyed if God did not the sooner cut short the days of that great scourge by his power. And for the protection of those who are chosen by him and whom he intends to keep, preserved and aided, he will destroy that arch-fiend and thenceforth will plunge him, and all the associates who followed him before and who believed his falsehoods too readily, into the depths of hell. Then God's judgement will be justly decided. And

indeed those then who love God and obey God's
laws, and eagerly attend to God's doctrines, and
keep them well, and resolutely persevere in true
faith to their life's end, these must gain eternal
reward in heavenly joy with God himself and with
his saints for evermore after the Judgement.
Eternal bliss is there, and ever shall be, world without end. Amen.

THE LAST DAYS

Both Ælfric and Wulfstan were in no doubt that their times
were the Last Days, but they had quite different approaches to
that perception. Ælfric's focus in his millennial preface to the
Catholic Homilies was on educating people to equip them to
face the persecution to come. Wulfstan was certainly concerned about education, but his focus and intention, even
when he was borrowing directly from Ælfric and from Adso,
was to confront people with the mess the world was in. He
developed the rhetoric of the list to a fine art, using alliteration and rhyme in the Old English version. In the penultimate
paragraph, for example, modern English only occasionally
seems to have the words to represent the driving impact of the
alliteration. And his impassioned style overflows in outbursts
of 'O!' and 'Lo', and questions, and repetitions of one of his
favourite tags, 'the longer things go on, the worse it gets'.
This is clearly a preacher writing for impact in oral delivery,
not, as Ælfric seems to be, for the effect of clear and balanced
argument.

That does not mean Wulfstan is not in control of his material. The quote from St Paul's second Epistle to Timothy is
adapted to Anglo-Saxon conditions. Paul writes to Timothy,
'There will be terrible times in the last days. People will be

lovers of themselves, lovers of money, boastful, proud ...
treacherous ... lovers of pleasure rather than lovers of God –
having the form of godliness but denying its power' (2
Timothy 3:1–5). Warriors in these times were supposed to
desire rewards, and be proud and boastful: this was part of the
war-ethic. But with it, they were also supposed to be loyal to
the death and protective especially towards the Church.
Wulfstan makes it clear that some have overdone the proud
and boastful side and underdone the loyal and protective side.
He goes on to remark several times on the decline of loyalty
among the people, both towards each other and towards the
Church. This is perhaps the overriding theme of Wulfstan's
works.

WULFSTAN AND THE VIKINGS

Just before Wulfstan became archbishop of York, King
Æthelred devised a plan to deal with the Viking threat. It
involved massacring the Scandinavians who were peacefully
living and trading in the country but not campaigning with
the Viking army. Some of the relatives of King Swein, the
Viking leader, were killed in this massacre, and he descended
on England in the years following 1002 with unprecedented
savagery. It was inevitable that Wulfstan should see his apoca-
lyptic predictions coming true: there were indeed terrible
persecutions coming. He maintained his view that the way to
resist was through loyalty to the faith, to the Church and
to each other. But he observed in a later and more famous
sermon, the *Sermo Lupi ad Anglos*, how his other prediction
that 'the longer things go on, the worse it gets' had also
come true.

He fills in the detail. Priests and religious people are
treated with contempt and church dues are no longer paid.

People sell each other into slavery; they buy slaves to subject them to gang-rape. They no longer defend their own family against abuse and indignity; they allow small numbers of enemies to take off many captives. And so on and on.

> It seems that here in this country there are too many injured by the ravages of sin. Here there are killers and kin-slayers and priest-murderers and persecutors of monasteries; here there are perjurers and murderers; here there are prostitutes and infanticides and many foul adulterous fornicators; here there are witches and valkyries; here are robbers and plunderers and ravagers, and to put it briefly, innumerable crimes and wickedness of all kinds. And we are not a bit ashamed of it, but it is evident among this wretched corrupt nation that we are more ashamed to begin the process of atonement as the books teach.

WULFSTAN AND POLITICS

King Swein's son, Cnut, became king of England in 1017 when Æthelred and his son Edmund died. Wulfstan helped the Scandinavian king to be reconciled with the English when it became evident that Cnut intended to stay and rule. A letter or proclamation from King Cnut to his subjects of about 1020 shows signs of being written by Wulfstan. What is especially interesting about this letter is that it could almost be a response to these sermons by Wulfstan. After the greeting, Cnut promises to be 'a loyal lord, maintaining God's rights and just secular law'. Starting from the top, Cnut is intending to set things right: law and order will be restored, justice will be done and be seen to be done; the people will

be defended from attack and from the abuse of power.
Specifically, the letter outlines, among other things:

> All the bishops say that oath-breaking and break-
> ing of pledges is to be deeply atoned for with God.
> And they also instruct us that we must with all
> our might and main inwardly seek, love and wor-
> ship the eternal, merciful God and turn away from
> all injustice: that is, from all kin-slayers and mur-
> derers and perjurers and witches and valkyries and
> adulterers and incestuous relations.

The proclamation shows Wulfstan's gift for listing sins and
sinners, and many of these are the same as those in the *Sermo
Lupi*. There is only one example in Old English of the use of
the word 'valkyrie' other than these two places. It seems to
mean someone who practises a kind of pagan witchcraft, and
the word is borrowed from Old Norse. So Cnut and his men
are as much being urged to turn away from heathenism as the
English. But these heathen and other sins are merely the
symptoms of a society where the ancient bonds of loyalty to
God and others have broken down. Set those right, Cnut and
Wulfstan seem to be saying, and the rest will follow; and to a
large degree, it did.

TEACHING AND INDIVIDUAL
TALENT

Ælfric and Wulfstan lived in perilous times indeed. They
approached maturity in the period following a time of peace
and prosperity under King Edgar, who died in 975. In the
years of their maturity, England descended into chaos as

Viking attacks disrupted Church and state, and law and order broke down. Ælfric had a major part to play in the education of the clergy and the laity, producing works which gave people access to basic Christian teaching in their own language. Wulfstan's role was more political. He read the signs of the times and exposed the rottenness at the core of English life, but was also instrumental in forming new laws, reaffirming old loyalties, and outlining the duties of king, Church and people. Both wrote homilies, and both were influential in reform. But the differences between them in temperament, approach and calling, enabled them to have influence in widely disparate lives and spheres, from the newest boy in the monastery to the king himself.

The Old English poem Almsgiving

It is well for the nobleman, a right-minded man,
who has within him a generous heart;
that is the greatest of dignities in the world for
    him,
and the best of honours before our Lord.
Even as one extinguishes the billowing flame
with water, so that, burning bright,
it can no longer damage cities,
so, by means of alms one can thrust aside
the wound of sins and heal souls.

It is possible that this poem is based on the first part of Psalm 41, 'Blessed is he who has regard for the weak; the Lord delivers him in times of trouble', and then on Ecclesiasticus 3:33, 'water quenches a fire, and alms resist sins'. Both Ælfric and Wulfstan were familiar with the billowing flame that damages cities, and both were convinced that spiritual and practical remedies were necessary for the sins of the times in which they were living. Alms-giving was as good a place as any to start the process of turning around the religious state of the country.

THE DRAMA OF THE
CHRISTIAN STORY

BOOKS AND READING

 The great events of the gospel story make wonderful reading. But most Anglo-Saxons either did not have access to books or could not read. Books were rare, and very costly and time-consuming to produce. Many were destroyed in the fighting and chances of history. While scholars might find this saddening, it has a surprising and cheering by-product. We find that the dramatic nature of some of the basic stories of the gospel has been enhanced in Christian tradition. Because those who *could* read, often read aloud for an audience, stories have been dramatized and the psychology of the characters has been explored.

LITURGY AND DRAMA

The Easter liturgy gave rise to the earliest known English drama, as the questions of the disciples and the answers of the angels at the tomb of Jesus were acted out, 'Whom do you seek in the tomb, O Christians?' But before that, the poets and homilists saw the dramatic potential of many of the stories. The story of the birth of Jesus is full of incident and excitement. Mary is visited by an angel and is told she will become miraculously pregnant. Joseph finds out about the pregnancy and decides to hush it up, before he is told by an angel to take Mary as his wife. Wonderful visitors guided by stars and angels pay honour to the child Jesus. The Nativity play of later years is there in the gospel stories, and the enchantment of it has found dramatic expression from time immemorial.

Mary's song, the Magnificat, about what God was doing by means of her child, appears in Luke 1:46–55, and it entered the liturgy of the Church. It expresses the hope of ordinary folk, that God in his Son will turn the worldly order of things on its head. The humble will be exalted and the powerful knocked down a peg or two. Poor old Joseph hardly features in the main events of the gospel story, but his plight was one that struck the Anglo-Saxons as uniquely difficult. How should an honourable man sort out the problems he faced?

The account of Joseph's quandary appears in Matthew 1:18–25.

This is how the birth of Jesus Christ came about. His mother Mary was pledged to be married to Joseph, but before they came together, she was found to be with child through the Holy Spirit. Because Joseph her husband was a righteous man and did not want to expose her to public disgrace, he had in mind to divorce her quietly.

But after he had considered this, an angel of the Lord appeared to him in a dream and said, 'Joseph, son of David, do not be afraid to take Mary home as your wife, because what is conceived in her is from the Holy Spirit. She will give birth to a son and you are to give him the name Jesus, because he will save his people from their sins.'

All this took place to fulfil what the Lord had said through the prophet: 'The virgin will be with child and will give birth to a son, and they will call him Immanuel' – which means 'God with us.'

When Joseph woke up, he did what the angel of the Lord had commanded him and took Mary home as his wife. But he had no union with her until she gave birth to a son. And he gave him the name Jesus.

THE OLD ENGLISH ADVENT

Among the traditional liturgical chants of Advent translated into Old English verse in the Exeter Book of Old English poetry, there is an imaginary dialogue between Mary and Joseph. It focuses on this episode and gives Joseph the chance to express his worries as well as letting Mary explain.

Mary:
O my Joseph, son of Jacob,
descendant of great King David,
must you now so strictly tear apart our affection,
and cut yourself off from my love?

Joseph:
    All at once I am
deeply upset and deprived of honour,
because I have heard many hurtful things about
    you:
much gossip, widespread anxiety,

bitter reproaches. And they insult me
and say angry things to me. I can only shed tears
in my misery. Only God is able to
heal the emotional pain in my heart
and comfort the miserable one. Oh, little girl,
maiden Mary!

Mary:
    What are you lamenting,
and why do you cry out with such anguish?
    I never found
fault in you, nor did I have any cause for complaint
about wrongs done. And you speak
as if you yourself were guilty of every sin
and full of defilement. I have had all too much
trouble from this pregnancy.

Joseph:
How can I clear myself of the hateful charges
or find any answer against
my enemies? It is widely known
that I willingly received a pure virgin
without stain at the bright
Temple of the Lord – and now that has all
    changed,
though how, I don't know. It does me no good
to speak or remain silent. If I tell the truth,
then a daughter of David's line must die,
put to death by stoning. But then it is worse
if I conceal the crime: then the pledge-breaker,
hateful to everyone, abominable among the
    people,
must live on.

Then the young woman revealed
the truth of the mystery, and said this:

Mary:
I am speaking the truth by the Son of God,
the Saviour of souls, that I have not yet slept
with any man anywhere on earth.
But it was granted to me,
still a child at home, that Gabriel,
archangel of heaven, should call to me in greeting.
He said truly that the light of the heavenly Spirit
would lighten upon me, and that I would bear the
    bright Son,
mighty child of God, life's power,
shining origin of glory. Now I am his temple,
built without sin; the Spirit of comfort has
taken up his home in me. So now give up
all your bitter lamenting. Give thanks for ever
to the glorious Son of God that I have become his
    mother,
though I am ever-virgin, and that you
will be called his father in the fashion of
    the world.

So, in his own Person,
had the prophecy [about Christ] to be
    truly fulfilled.

This is a deeply moving exchange. Mary is upset by Joseph's
decision to put her away, to break off their engagement, and
protests their love for each other. Confident and strong, she
knows that Joseph will be hurting himself if he shuts her out
of his life. But Joseph has to bear the burden of public shame

for both of them: he hears his love slandered and he himself blamed for her unseemly condition. In a moment of self-pity he wishes God to comfort him and feels compassion for the youth of his fiancée.

But again Mary is the more confident one. She brings him down to earth: look at the facts, not at what people are saying, she urges. '*I've* never said it was you who made me pregnant, and now you're talking as if you had, as if the things people blame you for were true. To be honest, this pregnancy is starting to get me down. Now I've got to comfort and encourage you as well.' 'That's all very well,' says Joseph, 'but look at it from the legal angle. Everybody knows that you were a virgin, and plainly now you are not. I don't know how it happened, and if I deny responsibility, then you are guilty of adultery and will be stoned. If I don't deny it publicly and legally, somebody gets off scot free, and I've got to live with the shame, and what everybody is saying about me.'

Then Mary tells her secret, and gives Joseph an account of the Annunciation. But whereas Gabriel had told her that the Holy Spirit would 'overshadow' her, she borrows the light metaphor of the beginning of John's gospel. Instead of being overshadowed, she is infused with light, she bears in her womb the light of the world. It is by the Holy Spirit that she has become pregnant, not by fornication. And she is reminded (anachronistically, but certainly) of St Paul's exhortations to the Corinthians, 'Flee from sexual immorality ... Do you not know that your body is a temple of the Holy Spirit, who is in you?' And as the Latin Vulgate Bible ends this chapter, 1 Corinthians 6, 'Glorify and bear God in your body'. So, very literally, she does. Mary also knows the traditional belief of the Catholic Church, that she remained a virgin even after the birth of her son. And finally she makes reference to Luke 3:23, which starts the genealogy of Jesus, 'he was the son, so it was thought, of Joseph': such is the fashion of the world.

REAL PROBLEMS

The dialogue gives Joseph the chance to explore the tricky problem confronting him. What the poet does is to imagine Joseph as an Anglo-Saxon as well as a Jewish man. As an honourable man he was concerned about his reputation. This was a vital matter to the Anglo-Saxons, for whom, in the words of one famous warrior, 'death is better than a life of shame'. Moreover, in Anglo-Saxon law it was relatively straightforward to resolve the problem of getting a girl pregnant. What was shameful was concealing the crime and giving the woman a bad name. So Joseph was in an unenviable position. The reply and final explanation from Mary clears all that away: it does not answer Joseph's particular problems, but instead reassures him and everybody else that God fulfils his purpose. She also teaches some useful lessons on the way.

This little dramatic interlude has no known direct source. There are passages in the apocryphal gospels and homilies of the Church which show similarities. But what the poet has done is to take the story and strip away the sentimental, liturgical and religious coating so that he can get at the real issues, the gritty awkwardness of life. The Holy Gospel and the Annunciation have become matters of love and guilt, confidence and fear, hope and misery. The poet has imagined the dilemmas of Joseph and Mary in their biblical context, but also put them into his own Anglo-Saxon context. He shows how confidence in God is the important thing. Both Mary and Joseph had that confidence, and through them indirectly, and Jesus directly, God's purpose was fulfilled.

This poem touches on the theological mysteries of the incarnation only in passing. The drama is intended to encourage Christians in their faith, and to deal with some of the objections the ignorant might have to the virgin birth. That this was a problem is evident from the glossing in the Lindisfarne Gospels. In the mid-10th century, a monk called Aldred felt compelled to note in his rather scrawly handwriting at Matthew 1:18 that Mary was betrothed, not married, to Joseph. The ability to see not only the dramatic possibilities of the biblical text, but also its relevance and application in a different culture, is not restricted to this poet, however. In a poem known as *The Dream of the Rood*, another poet explores the story of the crucifixion.

THE DRAMA OF THE CRUCIFIXION

The drama in *The Dream of the Rood* arises from the crucifixion of Jesus being seen not by a detached observer, but by a participant in the action. The strikingly original twist of the story is that it is told by the cross itself. And the cross is portrayed as a loyal retainer of his lord, who is forced by his loyalty and obedience to co-operate in killing that same lord. The fact that it sounds bizarre to talk of the psychology of the cross, the dilemmas and quandaries it experiences, is testimony to the originality of the device. The fact that the poet carries off this creative stroke of genius is testimony to his skill both as a poet and as a theologian.

The story is told to a man, in a dream, by the cross. The cross depicts himself as a warrior, but a warrior with a sad history; like the exiles of Old English poems, he has a tale to tell of suffering and trial, but one which has a happy ending.

The best of trees began to speak these words:
'That was a long time ago – I can still remember
      it –
when I was cut down at the edge of the wood,
removed from my stem. There strong enemies
      seized me,
made me a spectacle for themselves, ordered me to
      raise up their criminals;
warriors carried me there on their shoulders until
      they set me up on a hill,
many enemies fixed me there. Then I saw the Lord
      of humanity
hasten, with great zeal, when he wished to climb
      upon me.
I did not dare bend or break there,
go against the Lord's word, even when I saw
the surface of the earth shake. I could have killed
all the enemies, yet I stood firm.
Then the young hero who was God almighty
      stripped himself,
strong and resolute; he climbed up on the
      high gallows,
brave in the sight of many, when he wished to
      redeem humanity.
I trembled when the warrior embraced me, yet I
      did not dare bow to the earth,
fall flat on the ground, but I had to stand firm.
I was raised as a cross. I hung up the powerful king,
the Lord of the heavens, I did not dare bow down.
They pierced me with bloody nails, and the
      wounds are yet visible on me,
the gaping marks of malicious strokes: I did not
      dare harm any of them.

They abused us both together. I was absolutely
    drenched with blood
which spouted from the warrior's side after he sent
    on his spirit.
I have experienced many dreadful things
on that hill. I saw the Lord of hosts
savagely stretched out. Darkness covered
the bright radiance of the Lord's body,
covered it with clouds; shadow went forth,
dark under the clouds. All creation wept,
lamented the King's death. Christ was on the cross.
Then from afar men hurried
to the Prince. I gazed on it all.
I was overcome with sorrows, yet I bowed humbly
    to the hands of those men
with much courage. There they took almighty
    God down,
relieved him of that heavy torment. The warriors
    abandoned me
to stand drenched with moisture. I was wounded to
    death with arrows.
There they laid down the one weary of limb, they
    stood at head and feet,
and gazed on the Lord of heaven; and he rested
    there for a time,
weary after the great conflict. Then, in the sight of
    the killers,
the warriors made him a grave, carved it out of
    bright stone,
and put in it the Lord of victories. Then they sang
    a dirge,
miserable in the evening, when they, weary,
    wanted to go away

from the glorious Lord. He remained there with
   no company.
So, weeping, we stood there for a long time
fixed in place. The voice of warriors
faded away; the body went cold,
the gracious house of the spirit. Then we were
   cut down,
all of us were felled to the ground – that was a
   fearful thing!
We were buried in a deep pit. Yet the Lord's retain-
   ers
and friends heard of us.
They adorned me with gold and silver.
Now you have been able to hear, my beloved hero,
that I have experienced severe sorrows
from the deeds of the inhabitants of iniquity. Now
   the time has come
when people on earth and all this marvellous
   creation,
far and wide, honour me,
and pray to this sign. On me the Son of God
suffered for a time. Therefore, glorious now,
I tower under the heavens, and I am able to heal
each one in whom is fear towards me.
Formerly I was made into the severest of tortures,
most hateful to the people, before I opened
   to them,
to bearers of speech, the right way of life.

THE CROSS

The first thing we learn about the cross from his own mouth
is that he was defeated and made a slave by his enemies: he

was humiliated and made to do their horrible bidding. He became an executioner, like the gladiators of the Romans. But fear of enemies is suddenly replaced by awed fear of the energetic and noble warrior who makes a dramatic entrance at this point. This warrior has the right to command because he is Lord of all. Even the earth shakes as he comes on the scene. Every fibre of the cross's being is engaged in loyalty and obedience to this lord, as he makes it clear that he wants the cross to serve him. Yet the service the lord requires runs contrary to all the cross's instincts. The cross wants to do the heroic thing, to defend his lord, to lay about him and cut down all the enemies. But his lord asks him to stand firm. Standing firm with his lord means suffering with him, for this lord willingly embraces death.

Standing firm is what St Paul urges the Ephesian Christians to do in the spiritual battle (6:10–19, here quoted from the Latin Vulgate version): 'Put on the armour of God so that you may be able to stand against the deceits of the devil,' he writes, and urges twice more that they stand. The cross takes the armour of Christ himself in a literal and physical sense, while Christ strips himself of all warrior armour for this fight. Both are abused and mutilated, but the cross stands. He has done what his lord commanded, but by his very obedience he has become involved in the killing of his lord. His modest victory feels very like defeat.

LOSS AND LIFE

Grief and shame welcome the darkness that covers the dreadful scene as the lord, Christ, hangs on the gallows. And when that is past and all is apparently over, there is the wearisome and dismal job of burying the lord and disposing of the cross. After the intensity of the action, the slow ebbing of energy, light, life-warmth and the sound of human voices, echoes the failure of hope. Then the cross is cut down, repeating the earlier brutal cutting down of the tree which became the cross, and he is buried in a deep pit. And that is the end of the business. Or so it would have been if that had been the end of the Lord.

But as Christ was raised up from death, so the cross is raised from the pit. And once this great coup has been achieved, the cross becomes a messenger telling the story. The focus moves away from the cross to the truths that it stands for. The cross still uses the personal pronouns to talk about its involvement in the drama, but it becomes clear that the cross has now changed its role, and it has become less of a participant and more of a symbol, pointing to Christ. It is honoured in its physicality by the followers of Christ as they cover it with gold and gems, but it is honoured too, spiritually, by every Christian. It speaks with confidence of its role in the drama of salvation, and it towers in its glory. The cross now revels in, and reveals, the ultimate, universal triumph of his Lord.

> Listen – the Lord of glory, the guardian of the
>   kingdom of heaven,
> then honoured me over the trees of the forest,
> just as he honoured Mary herself,
> his mother, before all people,
> God almighty honoured her above all the race of
>   women.
> Now I command you, my beloved hero,
> that you tell this vision to people,
> reveal in words that it is the tree of glory
> on which almighty God suffered
> for the many sins of humankind
> and for Adam's deeds of old.

He tasted death there, yet the Lord rose again
by his mighty power to aid all people.
He then ascended to the heavens. He, the Lord
   himself,
God almighty, and his angels with him,
will come back here to this earth
to seek mankind on the day of judgement,
when he, the one who had the right to judge,
wishes to judge each one according
to what they have earned in this passing life.

The poem takes us from the specific events of Easter seen and experienced through the cross, to the general application of theological truth in the Creed, as echoed in these lines. It models the response that it expects from Christians hearing the story: moving from personal involvement in the drama of salvation, to worship for the Saviour. This is a specific aim of the liturgy of the Church, and it is as a companion to the liturgy that the poem's drama works best.

LITURGY

Throughout, the words and phrases of the poem echo and amplify the liturgy. The liturgical Easter hymns of Venantius Fortunatus, Bishop of Poitiers in the later sixth century, give a hint of where the poet got his inspiration from. The two hymns below, *Pange lingua* and *Vexilla regis*, are given in the translation by J.M. Neale in *Medieval Hymns*. The first of these dwells on the role of the cross as *The Dream of the Rood* does:

Sing, my tongue, the glorious battle,
With completed victory rife:
And above the Cross's trophy
Tell the triumph of the strife:
How the world's Redeemer conquer'd
By surrendering of His Life...

Faithful Cross! above all other,
One and only noble tree!
None in foliage, none in blossom,
None in fruit thy peers may be:
Sweetest Wood, and sweetest Iron!
Sweetest Weight is hung on thee.

Bend thy boughs, O Tree of glory!
Thy relaxing sinews bend;
For awhile the ancient rigour,
That thy birth bestowed, suspend;
And the King of Heavenly Beauty
On thy bosom gently tend!

Thou alone wast counted worthy
This world's ransom to uphold;
For a shipwrecked race preparing
Harbour, like the Ark of old;
With the sacred Blood anointed
From the smitten LAMB that roll'd...

The cross is personified in the hymn, and honoured for
its faithfulness. It is exalted above all trees because it was
anointed by the blood of Christ. In all these things, the Old
English poem is following the lead of the hymn. In both the
hymn and *The Dream of the Rood* the paradoxes of victory in

defeat and glory in suffering are explored. *The Dream* takes the ideas further by giving the personified cross its own voice, a device used in the Old English riddles; and by making its experience that of an Old English warrior. These naturalize the drama, and make the cross's dilemmas accessible to the Old English audience, as well as helping them to understand and appreciate the liturgy.

It is the flickering contrasts in the cross's appearance that make the dreamer in the Old English poem fearful. As he sees it, the cross is both wonderful and yet sinister:

> Listen. I want to describe the best of dreams
> that came to me in the middle of the night
> when humans capable of speech kept their beds.
> It seemed to me that I saw a superb tree,
> brightest of trees, caught up in the clouds,
> surrounded with light. All that sign was
> drenched with gold, gems gleamed
> gracious at the surface of the earth, and similarly
>   there were five
> up on the cross-beam. Armies of angels, beautiful
>   from first creation,
> gazed there; that was surely not the gallows
>   of a felon,
> but the spirits of the holy ones, people on earth,
> and all this marvellous creation gazed upon
>   it there.
> Wondrous was the tree of victory, and I was
>   stained with sins,
> injured by iniquities. I saw the tree of glory
> graced with garments, joyously shining,
> adorned with gold. Jewels nobly
> covered the tree of the Lord.

Yet through the gold, I was able to perceive
the ancient strife of enemies, when it began for the
   first time
to bleed on the right hand side. I was devastated
   with sorrows,
afraid because of the beautiful vision. I saw the
   shimmering sign
change colour and garments: sometimes it was
   dripping with wetness,
drenched with the flow of blood; sometimes it was
   adorned with treasure.
So lying there for a long time, I gazed, sorrowing,
upon the Saviour's tree,
until I heard that it spoke.

The cross is impressive here, a processional cross held high,
tied with white festive streamers, an Easter cross. Yet it is also
the rough cross of Good Friday, stained with blood, tied with
red streamers, symbol of strife and suffering. It is the predominantly glorious cross that appears in *Vexilla regis*:

> The Royal Banners forward go;
> The Cross shines forth in mystic glow;
> Where He in flesh, our flesh Who made,
> Our sentence bore, our ransom paid.

> Where deep for us the spear was dy'd,
> Life's torrent rushing from His side,
> To wash us in that precious flood
> Where mingled Water flow'd, and Blood.

> Fulfill'd is all that David told
> In true prophetic song of old;

Amidst the nations GOD, saith he,
Hath reign'd and triumph'd from the Tree.

O Tree of Beauty! Tree of Light!
O Tree with royal purple dight!
Elect on whose triumphal breast
Those holy limbs should find their rest!

On whose dear arms, so widely flung,
The weight of this world's ransom hung:
The price of human kind to pay,
And spoil the Spoiler of his prey.

The Fortunatus hymns were used mostly on the festivals of the cross and at Easter. They celebrate the cross as the means by which Christ secured salvation. Fortunatus implies the horror of crucifixion only very obliquely in these hymns, preferring to concentrate on the paradoxical glory of the cross. By giving the cross its own voice, the poet of *The Dream of the Rood* brings these liturgical hymns and the gospels closer together. The gospels tell the story, with little interpretation. *The Dream* gives both story and interpretation. Suffering and glory are given equal weight; Christ's blood is from real wounds, causing real pain, as well as 'Life's torrent', the means of salvation. The drama of this poem takes us from the religious liturgy of celebration, through a sense of unease in the dreamer, through the dreadful experiences of the cross, back to the religious liturgy. Once again the patina of religious familiarity is stripped off, leaving us to experience the raw emotions of the Easter story, and to come back to worship with a fresh understanding of the cost, and value, of the salvation symbolized by the cross.

THE ATONEMENT AND THE HARROWING OF HELL

The final lines of the hymn as quoted above are rather elliptical in the original Latin, meaning something like, 'The cross was made the balance [on which] his body [was weighed against sin], and [by the sacrifice of the cross, he] carried off the booty of hell'. The idea is that in the scales of justice, Christ's sacrifice was worth more than human sin, and by paying more than human sin, he was able to pay the debt of those who had gone to hell. He thus ransomed the captives of the devil in hell. *The Dream of the Rood* ends on the high heroic note of the harrowing of hell:

> He redeemed us, gave us life
> and a heavenly home. Hope was renewed
> gloriously and blissfully, for those who endured
>   burning there:
> the Son was victorious on that expedition,
> powerful and successful, when he came with
>   a host,
> a whole troop of spirits, into God's kingdom,
> the almighty sole ruler, to the bliss of angels
> and all the holy ones who formerly had dwelt
>   in heaven
> and remained in glory, when their Lord,
>   almighty God,
> came back to where his home was.

This theme is common in Old English literature. In a poem called *Christ and Satan*, the poet develops a sustained contrast between heaven and hell, but in one section of the poem he explores the drama of Christ's conquest of hell. In relatively few lines, and concentrating on the harrowing of hell, the poet nevertheless manages to encapsulate the whole of Christian history. We start with the fall of the angels.

That angel who has been named before
was called Lucifer, 'the light-bearer',
in the old days in God's kingdom.
But then he stirred up strife in heaven
because he wished to indulge in pride.
Then Satan darkly conceived the desire
that he would build a hall in heaven
on high alongside the eternal One. Satan was the
    leader of them all,
the prime mover of evil. He regretted that
when he had to sink down to hell,
fall into humiliation and into the Saviour's enmity,
along with his followers. Never afterwards,
for ever without end, would they be allowed
to see the face of the eternal One. Then horror
    came upon them,
outcry because of the Judge, when he
    smashed down
the gates in hell. Joy came over the people there
when they saw the Saviour's head,
more than came upon the terrible ones we
    mentioned earlier.
Then all throughout the entire windswept hall
were struck with horror, and made this lament:
'This is hard to endure, now the warrior with
    his army,
the Prince of the angels, has arrived, with this
    uproar.
Before him goes a more beautiful light

than we ever saw with our own eyes before,
except when we were on high with the angels.
The torments we inflict he now intends to
 cast aside
by the power of his glory! Now this horror has
 come upon us,
outcry because of the Lord, this miserable horde
must now soon suffer terror.
It is the Son of the Ruler himself,
the Lord of the angels! He intends to take
 the souls
away on high, and ever afterwards
we will suffer the humiliation of that defeat.'
The Creator by his own power went to hell then,
to the children of men. He intended to lead forth
a multitude of people, many thousands,
up to his homeland. Then came the song of angels,
loud at daybreak: the Lord himself
had defeated the enemy, and the hostility was still
evident in the light of dawn, when the horror
 came upon them.
He made the blessed souls of Adam's descendants
rise up on high.
 But Eve could not let herself
gaze upon glory before she said these words:
'Eternal Lord, I once offended you
when, through the malice of the serpent,
Adam and I ate the apple as we ought not to have
 done.
The terrible one, who now forever burns in chains,
assured us that we would have honour,
a holy home, and heaven in our control.
So we believed the accursed one's words,

and took the bright fruit from the holy tree
with our hands. We were bitterly repaid
when we had to come to this hot cave
and afterwards spend years and years,
thousands of years, being cruelly burned.
Now I implore you, Guardian of the kingdom
    of heaven,
in the presence of this army that you brought here,
the hosts of angels, that I might be allowed
    and able
to ascend on high with my descendants.
Three nights ago, a former thane of the
    Saviour came
home to hell (he is now in strong bonds
and enduring torments because of his pride,
just as the King of glory in his wrath ordained
    for him).
He told us truly that God himself
intended to come down to the home of hell-
    dwellers.
Each one got up, raising themselves with an
    arm and
leaned on their elbow: though the torment of hell
seemed terrible to them, they were all
cheered by this in their sufferings – that the Lord
intended to come to hell to help them.'
She reached out with her hands to the King
    of heaven,
and asked the Creator for mercy by her relation
    with Mary:
'Lo, you were born into the world, Lord,
through my daughter, coming to the aid of
    humans.

Now it is clear that you are God himself,
the eternal Originator of all created things.'

The source of this poem is the apocryphal *Gospel of Nicodemus*, and it reveals the common medieval understanding of the atonement, how Christ saved humankind. In this view, all those who sinned before Christ went to hell. Christ offered himself to the devil in exchange for them, was killed, and descended into hell. But hell and the devil could not hold him, and after three days he ascended, and took with him all the souls of the righteous from hell. The Old English poem sees this as a heroic victory.

THE DRAMA OF RESCUE

The poet sets the scene with the fall of the angels. Satan the 'light-bearer' falls from heaven because of his dark thoughts. Denied the light of God's face, the fallen angels fear the beautiful light that precedes Christ's coming, and the dawn which reveals his victory. But what is bad news for the demons is good news for the souls in hell, who, in Eve's words, wearily raise themselves up on their elbows to welcome the news of help.

The three speeches tell the story and reveal the characters of the speakers. The light the demons see as Christ approaches reminds them of what they once were, and the reversal of their nature that has taken place as angels have become demons. They lament another reversal: that their power to inflict torment on human souls is about to come to an end, and they instead will suffer humiliation.

Then comes the decisive move of Christ, accompanied by light and song, as he takes the souls home to heaven, where they belong. But Eve feels the need to explain her reluctance, her unease at going to heaven, feeling perhaps the guilt of her part in the suffering of the souls in hell. She tells the story of the fall in the Garden of Eden, and how human beings became tainted with sin and went inevitably to hell to suffer over the interminable years. Then she tells how the messenger came to hell, perhaps gleeful, with the news that Christ was being killed, and how even this cheered the dismal souls. She leaves the story hanging, because the three days are over and hell has been despoiled. She reaches out her hands, pleading that as she shares in Christ's humanity through the special relationship of motherhood through Mary, so she might share his mercy as he is revealed to be God incarnate.

TOUCHING THE HEART

The story is concisely and vividly told. The account is shot through with theology, without being burdened by it. The emotions of the characters are made visible and believable. Eve's speeches in particular explore the sense of unworthiness that people sometimes feel before God. Yet she reaches out, in worship, claiming her kinship with Christ. The story justifies the ways of God by dramatizing them, but Eve's gesture touches the mystery at the heart of it all. Human beings reach out to Christ who shares their nature, yet is God himself.

An Old English version of the Creed

I believe in God the Father almighty.
Almighty Father, up in the sky,
who made and shaped the bright creation
and established all the plains of the earth,
I acknowledge and willingly trust you alone,
eternal God. You are the Lord of life,
the origin of the angels, the Ruler of earth,
and you made the depths of the oceans,
and know the multitude of the glorious stars.
And in Jesus Christ his only Son our Lord.
I trust in your true Son,
Saviour King, the One sent here
from the realm of the angels above,
the One Gabriel, God's messenger
announced to holy Mary herself.
A pure young woman, she received that message
nobly, and in her womb she bore
you, Son of the Father, yourself.
No sin was committed at the conception,
but the Holy Spirit gave a wedding-gift
which filled the virgin's bosom with joy.
And she knowingly bore for the inhabitants of
    the earth
the glorious Creator of the angels,
the One who came as a comfort to dwellers on
    earth.
And around Bethlehem, the angels
proclaimed that Christ was born on earth.
He suffered under Pontius Pilate.
When Pontius Pilate had power

over the kingdom and over justice under
  the Romans,
then the dear Lord suffered death.
He, the Lord of warriors, mounted up on
  the gallows;
sad in heart, Joseph buried him;
and he brought back booty from hell,
that hall of torture, many souls,
and commanded them to go to their home above.
On the third day he rose again from death.
The third day after the Ruler, Lord of the kingdom,
rose again quickly from the earth.
And for 40 days comforted his followers
with divine mysteries. And then
he sought the home above.
He said that he had no intention of abandoning
  anyone
who wished to follow him thereafter
and who with firm mind wished to commit
  themselves to him in love.
I believe in the Holy Spirit.
I hold as my hope the Holy Spirit,
co-eternal with the Father and the noble Son,
just as each of them is said to be by the voice of
  the people.
These are not three gods, invoked three times
  by name,
but it is one God who has all three names
in the mysteries of his nature,
true and glorious throughout the wide creation,
the giver of glory to the hosts, high and eternal.
And in the holy catholic church.
And I also believe that they are dear to God
who through resolute intent worship the Lord,
the high King of heaven, here in this life.

And in the communion of saints.
And I believe in the glorious fellowship
of your saints, here in this life.
The forgiveness of sins.
I believe in the forgiveness of every sin.
The resurrection of the body.
And I believe in the resurrection of all,
every body on earth, in that fearful time –
And the life eternal.
– where you will give eternal life to all,
just as each person is pleasing to the Ruler.

Here is the full drama of the Christian story, all the themes of creation, incarnation, crucifixion, descent into hell, resurrection, the Trinity and the rest. But the theological vocabulary of that list masks the sure and homely touch of the poet. He has Mary receiving a 'wedding-gift', the gift that a man gave a woman after the consummation of their marriage. He has Joseph of Arimathea burying the body of Jesus after he has been on the 'gallows', where the gallows, as in *The Dream of the Rood*, is the place of execution familiar to the Anglo-Saxons. He has Jesus bringing back 'booty' from hell, just as the warriors would bring back the spoil after a battle, if they survived. He has Jesus send the souls he has freed 'home', to where they belong, where they are loved and cherished in heaven. And he goes home himself after comforting his followers. These are the things that show a poet who lives in a Christian world which he has made his own. The Creed is truly his *credo*, 'I believe', not just belief, vague and general.

CONCLUSION

We have covered a lot of ground in the chapters of this book. Stories and poems and prayers and sermons have laid bare the thoughts and experiences of the Anglo-Saxons. There has been a mixture of emotions, joy and sorrow, serenity and anxiety. We may have shared some of the particular experiences that the Anglo-Saxons had, and some experiences we can only enter into by sympathy. Yet threading it all is a sense that, despite the superficial differences of culture and society, we can learn something from them. Their practical spirituality, unaffected, robust, profound and honest, always impresses me. Their learning, with desperately limited resources, amazes me. Their courage in the face of loss and their creativity in the face of ordinariness is a challenge to me.

I hope my reactions to the Anglo-Saxons and their faith might stimulate thought and response on the part of my readers. But above all, I hope that this book will have refreshed and rewarded readers with a deeper understanding of the ancient and ever new Christian faith, and the God whose idea it was in the first place.

SOURCES AND
FURTHER READING

Sources are given according to the order that the texts appear in the chapters.

Texts of Old English poems are my own, translated throughout from Krapp, George Philip, and Elliott Van Kirk Dobbie, ed., *The Anglo-Saxon Poetic Records: A Collective Edition*, 6 vols, New York, Columbia University Press, 1931–42.

The Bible is quoted, except where noted, from the *Holy Bible, New International Version*, © 1973, 1978, 1984 by International Bible Society. Used by permission of Hodder & Stoughton Ltd, a member of the Hodder Headline Plc Group. All rights reserved.

GENERAL

BACKGROUND HISTORY
Blair, Peter Hunter, *An Introduction to Anglo-Saxon England*, 2nd edn, Cambridge, Cambridge University Press, 1977
Campbell, James, ed., *The Anglo-Saxons*, London, Penguin Books, 1991
Godfrey, John, *The Church in Anglo-Saxon England*, Cambridge, Cambridge University Press, 1962
Stenton, F.M., *Anglo-Saxon England*, 3rd edn, Oxford, The Oxford History of England vol. 2, Clarendon Press, 1971

Anglo-Saxon literature translated from Latin and Old English:

Whitelock, D., ed., *English Historical Documents Vol. I, c. 500–1042*, 3rd edn, London, Eyre Methuen, 1979

Cavill, P., *Anglo-Saxon Christianity*, London, Fount, 1999, and *Vikings: Fear and Faith*, London, HarperCollins, 2001

General literary studies, essay collections:

Aertsen, Henk and Rolf H. Bremmer, ed., *Companion to Old English Poetry*, Amsterdam, VU University Press, 1994

Godden, Malcolm, and Michael Lapidge, ed., *The Cambridge Companion to Old English Literature*, Cambridge, Cambridge University Press, 1991

Stanley, E.G., ed., *Continuations and Beginnings: Studies in Old English Literature*, London, Nelson, 1966

CHAPTER 1

ÆLFRIC'S SERMONS

Thorpe, Benjamin, ed. and trans., *The Homilies of the Anglo-Saxon Church: The First Part, Containing the Sermones Catholici or Homilies of Ælfric*, 2 vols, London, Ælfric Society, 1844–6; the translation of Ælfric's 'Beginning of the Creation' is taken from Thorpe, I, pp. 8–29.

Clemoes, Peter, ed., *Ælfric's Catholic Homilies: The First Series Text*, Oxford, Early English Text Society Supplementary Series vol. 17, Oxford University Press, 1997

Godden, Malcolm, ed., *Ælfric's Catholic Homilies: The Second Series Text*, London, Early English Text Society Supplementary Series vol. 5, Oxford University Press, 1979

THE *DURHAM HYMNAL*

Milfull, Inge B., ed., *The Hymns of the Anglo-Saxon Church: A Study and Edition of the 'Durham Hymnal'*, Cambridge Studies in Anglo-Saxon England 17, Cambridge University Press, 1996

'O COME, O COME IMMANUEL'

Neale, J.M., trans., *Mediæval Hymns and Sequences*, 3rd edn, London, Joseph Masters, 1867

THE *LIVES* OF ST CUTHBERT
Colgrave, Bertram, ed. and trans., *Two Lives of Saint Cuthbert*,
   Cambridge, Cambridge University Press, 1940

CHAPTER 2

BALD'S LEECHBOOK
Cockayne, Thomas O., ed. and trans., *Leechdoms, Wortcunning, and
   Starcraft of Early England*, 3 vols, Rolls series, London 1864–6;
   vol. II

HILD
Colgrave, B. and, R.A.B. Mynors, ed. and trans., *Bede's Ecclesiastical
   History of the English People*, Oxford, Oxford Medieval Texts,
   Clarendon Press, 1969; Book IV, 23–4

RECTITUDINES SINGULARUM PERSONARUM AND OTHER LAWS
Liebermann, F., *Die Gesetze der Angelsachsen*, 3 vols, Max Niemeyer,
   Tübingen, 1898–1903

THE COLLOQUY
Garmonsway, G.N., ed., *Ælfric's Colloquy*, rev. edn by Swanton,
   M.J., Exeter, Exeter University Press, 1991

THE LINDISFARNE GOSPELS
Backhouse, Janet, *The Lindisfarne Gospels*, Oxford, Phaidon, 1981
Kendrick, T.D., T.J. Brown, and R.L.S. Bruce-Mitford, ed.,
   Euangeliorum quattuor Codex Lindisfarnensis, 2 vols, Lausanne,
   1960 (facsimile)

THE LORD'S PRAYER AND THE OTHER LITURGICAL POEMS AND
PROSE
Ure, James, ed., *The Benedictine Office*, Edinburgh, Edinburgh
   University Press, 1957

GENERAL
Page, R.I., *Life in Anglo-Saxon England*, London, English Life series,
   B.T. Batsford, 1970

CHAPTER 3

THE WANDERER, THE SEAFARER AND OTHER POEMS OF EXILE
Klinck, Anne L., ed., *The Old English Elegies: A Critical Edition and
Genre Study*, Montreal, McGill-Queen's University Press, 1992

ÆLFRIC'S GRAMMAR
Zupitza, Julius, ed., *Ælfrics Grammatik und Glossar*, Berlin,
Weidmannsche Buchhandlung, 1880

C.S. LEWIS
Lewis, C.S., *A Grief Observed*, London, Faber, 1961

CHAPTER 4

KING EDMUND'S LAWS
see Liebermann, chapter 2 above

THE DURHAM PROVERBS
Arngart, Olof, ed., *The Durham Proverbs*, Lund, Lunds Universitets
Årsskrift, 1956, and 'The Durham Proverbs', rev. edn, *Speculum*,
56 (1981), 288–300

THE OLD ENGLISH *DICTS OF CATO*
Cox, R.S., ed., 'The Old English Dicts of Cato', *Anglia*, 90 (1972),
1–42

WULFSTAN
Bethurum, Dorothy, ed., *The Homilies of Wulfstan*, Oxford,
Clarendon Press, 1957; from the homily *De septiformi spiritu*, no.
IX in Bethurum's collection

KING ALFRED'S BOETHIUS
Sedgefield, Walter John, ed., *King Alfred's Old English Version of
Boethius, De Consolatione Philosophiae*, Oxford, Clarendon Press,
1899
Fox, Samuel, ed. and trans., *King Alfred's Anglo-Saxon Version of
Boethius De Consolatione Philosophiae*, London, Bohn's
Antiquarian Library, 1864

WISDOM LITERATURE IN GENERAL
Cavill, Paul, *Maxims in Old English Poetry*, Cambridge, D.S. Brewer, 1999

CHAPTER 5

BEDE'S *ECCLESIASTICAL HISTORY*
see Colgrave and Mynors, chapter 2 above

BEDE'S *HISTORY OF THE ABBOTS*
Plummer, Charles, ed., *Venerabilis Baedae Opera Historica*, 2 vols, Oxford, Clarendon Press, 1896; I, pp. 364–87

THE 'MONASTIC AGREEMENT'
Symons, Thomas, ed., *Regularis Concordia*, London, Nelson's Medieval Texts, Nelson, 1953

OLD ENGLISH CHARTERS
Robertson, A.J., ed., *Anglo-Saxon Charters*, Cambridge, Cambridge University Press, 1939
Colloquy: see Garmonsway, chapter 2 above
The Benedictine Office: see Ure, chapter 2 above

CHAPTER 6

CUTHBERT'S LETTER
see Colgrave and Mynors, chapter 2 above
Anonymous *Life* of Ceolfrid, *History of the Abbots*: see Plummer, chapter 5 above; I, pp. 388–404

ALCUIN'S LETTER ABOUT BEDE
Haddan, A.W. and W. Stubbs, *Councils and Ecclesiastical Documents Relating to Great Britain and Ireland*, 3 vols, Oxford, Clarendon Press, 1869, repr. 1964; III, pp. 470–71

THE LETTERS OF BONIFACE
Dümmler, E., ed., *Monumenta Germaniae Historica, Epistolae Tomus III, Bonifatii et Lulli Epistolae*, Berlin, 1892

Emerton, Ephraim, trans., *The Letters of Saint Boniface*, New York, Records of Civilization 31, Columbia University Press, 1940; the letter to Archbishop Ecgberht is quoted from Emerton's translation, p. 168

ESSAYS ON BEDE

Bonner, G., ed., *Famulus Christi: Essays in Commemoration of the Thirteenth Centenary of the Birth of the Venerable Bede*, London, SPCK, 1976

Thompson, A. Hamilton, ed., *Bede, His Life, Times and Writings*, Oxford, Oxford University Press, 1935; the passage from Bede's commentary on Revelation is quoted from Claude Jenkins's essay in this collection, 'Bede as exegete and theologian', p. 153

Ward, B., *The Venerable Bede*, London, Geoffrey Chapman, 1990

BEDE'S COMMENTARY ON SAMUEL

Hurst, D., ed., *Bedae Venerabilis opera, Opera exegetica, In primam partem Samuhelis libri IIII*, Turnhout, *Corpus Christianorum series latina* CXIX, Brepols, 1962

BEDE'S COMMENTARY ON JAMES

Laistner, M.L.W., ed., *Bedae Venerabilis opera, Opera exegetica, In epistolas VII catholicas*, Turnhout, *Corpus Christianorum series latina* CXXI, Brepols, 1983

BEDE'S COMMENTARY ON LUKE

Hurst, D., ed., *Bedae Venerabilis opera, Opera exegetica, In Lucam*, Turnhout, *Corpus Christianorum series latina* CXX, Brepols, 1960

BEDE ON THE TABERNACLE

Hurst, D., ed., *Bedae Venerabilis opera, Opera exegetica, De tabernaculo*, Turnhout, *Corpus Christianorum series latina* CXIXA, Brepols, 1969

Holder, Arthur G., trans., *Bede: On the Tabernacle*, Liverpool, Translated Texts for Historians vol. 18, Liverpool University Press, 1994; the section given is from Holder, pp. 81–2

BEDE ON CÆDMON

see Colgrave and Mynors, chapter 2 above

BEDE ON TIMES

Jones, C.W., ed., *Bedae Opera de Temporibus*, Cambridge MA, The Mediaeval Academy of America, 1943

Wallis, Faith, trans., *Bede: The Reckoning of Time*, Liverpool, Translated Texts for Historians vol. 29, Liverpool University Press, 1999

CHAPTER 7

SAINTS AND THEIR CULTS

Brown, Peter, *The Cult of the Saints*, London, SCM Press, 1981

Delehaye, Hippolyte, trans. Attwater, Donald, *The Legends of the Saints*, London, Chapman, 1962

Farmer, David Hugh, *The Oxford Dictionary of Saints*, 3rd edn, Oxford, Oxford University Press, 1992

Woolf, Rosemary, 'Saints' Lives' in Stanley, above

THE *LIFE* OF BISHOP WILFRID

Colgrave, Bertram, ed. and trans., *The Life of Bishop Wilfrid by Eddius Stephanus*, Cambridge, Cambridge University Press, 1927

Kirby, D.P., ed., *Saint Wilfrid at Hexham*, Newcastle, Oriel Press, 1974

CUTHBERT

see Colgrave, *Two Lives*, chapter 1 above, and further, chapter 8 below

HILD

see Colgrave and Mynors above

ST NICHOLAS

Treharne, E.M., *The Old English Life of St Nicholas with the Old English Life of St Giles*, Leeds, Leeds Texts and Monographs, new series 15, 1997

ST GUTHLAC

Colgrave, Bertram, ed. and trans., *Felix's Life of Saint Guthlac*, Cambridge, Cambridge University Press, 1956

ST ÆTHELTHRYTH
see Colgrave and Mynors above

GREGORY THE GREAT
Colgrave, Bertram, ed. and trans., *The Earliest Life of Gregory the Great*, repr. Cambridge, Cambridge University Press, 1985

GREGORY'S LETTER TO ST AUGUSTINE
see Colgrave and Mynors above

ST ÆTHELWOLD
Lapidge, Michael and Michael Winterbottom, ed. and trans., *Wulfstan of Winchester: The Life of St Æthelwold*, Oxford, Clarendon Press, 1991
Yorke, Barbara, ed., *Bishop Æthelwold: His Career and Influence*, Woodbridge, Boydell, 1988

ÆLFRIC ON ST OSWALD
Skeat, Walter W., ed. and trans., *Ælfric's Lives of Saints: Being a Set of Sermons on Saints' Days Formerly Observed by the English Church*, 2 vols, London, Early English Text Society Original Series vols 76, 82, 94 and 114, Oxford University Press, 1881–1900, repr. 1966
Latin hymn from the *Durham Hymnal*: see Milfull above; the translation is from Milfull, pp. 359–60

CHAPTER 8

ESSAYS ON ST CUTHBERT
Bonner, Gerald, Clare Stancliffe, and David Rollason, ed., *St Cuthbert: His Cult and His Community to A.D 1200*, Woodbridge, Boydell, 1989

THE *LIVES* OF ST CUTHBERT
see Colgrave, *Two Lives*, chapter 1 above

BEDE'S SUMMARY IN THE *ECCLESIASTICAL HISTORY*
see Colgrave and Mynors, chapter 2 above

SYMEON OF DURHAM'S STORY ABOUT ST CUTHBERT

Rollason, David, ed. and trans., *Symeon of Durham: Libellus de Exordio atque Procursu istius hoc est Dunhelmensis Ecclesie*, Oxford, Oxford Medieval Texts, Clarendon Press, 2000

Latin hymn from the *Durham Hymnal*: see Milfull above; the translation is from Milfull, p. 254

CHAPTER 9

ROMAN HISTORIANS AND OTHER EARLY REFERENCES TO PERSECUTION

Stevenson, J., ed. and trans., *A New Eusebius: Documents Illustrative of the History of the Church to AD 337*, London, SPCK, 1957

THE OLD ENGLISH MARTYROLOGY

Herzfeld, George, ed., *An Old English Martyrology*, London, Early English Text Society Original Series 116, Oxford University Press, 1900

ÆLFRIC ON ST ALBAN

see Skeat, chapter 7 above

ST EDMUND

Hervey, Lord Francis, ed. and trans., *Corolla Sancti Eadmundi: The Garland of Saint Edmund King and Martyr*, London, John Murray, 1907

Winterbottom, M., *Three Lives of English Saints*, Toronto, Toronto Medieval Latin Texts, 1972 (the most recent edn of the *Passio sancti Eadmundi Regis et Martyris* by Abbo of Fleury)

A GENERAL STUDY OF ANGLO-SAXON ROYAL SAINTS

Ridyard, Susan J., *The Royal Saints of Anglo-Saxon England: A Study of West Saxon and East Anglian Cults*, Cambridge, Cambridge Studies in Medieval Life and Thought, Cambridge University Press, 1988

ST EDWARD

Fell, Christine E., ed., *Edward King and Martyr*, Leeds, University of Leeds School of English, 1971

Mynors, R.A.B., R.M. Thomson, and M. Winterbottom, ed. and trans., *William of Malmesbury: Gesta Regum Anglorum*, vol. 1, Oxford, Oxford Medieval Texts, Clarendon Press, 1998

WULFSTAN'S *SERMO LUPI AD ANGLOS*
see Bethurum, chapter 4 above

THE *ANGLO-SAXON CHRONICLE*
Plummer, Charles, ed., *Two of the Saxon Chronicles Parallel: ... On the Basis of an Edition by John Earle*, 2 vols, Oxford, Clarendon Press, 1892–99, reissued with a bibliographical note by D. Whitelock, 1952

OSBERN'S LIFE OF ÆLFHEAH
Wharton, H., ed., *De Sancto Elphego Martyre*, in *Anglia Sacra*, 2 vols, London, 1691

ANSELM AND LANFRANC
Southern, R.W., ed. and trans., *The Life of St Anselm, Archbishop of Canterbury by Eadmer*, Oxford, Oxford Medieval Texts, Clarendon Press, 1962

LATIN PRAYER FOR THE FEAST OF ST EDMUND
Muir, Bernard James, ed., *A Pre-Conquest English Prayer-Book (BL MSS Cotton Galba A.xiv and Nero A.ii)*, Woodbridge, Henry Bradshaw Society vol. 103, Boydell, 1988, p. 182

CHAPTER 10

GENERAL DISCUSSION OF ÆLFRIC AND WULFSTAN
Gatch, Milton McC., *Preaching and Theology in Anglo-Saxon England: Ælfric and Wulfstan*, Toronto, University of Toronto Press, 1977

MILLENNIALISM
Godden, Malcolm, 'Apocalypse and invasion in late Anglo-Saxon England' in Godden, Malcolm, Douglas Gray and Terry Hoad, ed., *From Anglo-Saxon to Middle English: Studies Presented to E.G. Stanley*, Oxford, Clarendon Press, 1994, pp. 130–62

ÆLFRIC'S PREFACES
Wilcox, Jonathan, ed., *Ælfric's Prefaces*, Durham, Durham Medieval Texts vol. 9, 1994

WULFSTAN'S HOMILIES
see Bethurum, chapter 4 above

WULFSTAN'S LAW CODES
see Liebermann, chapter 2 above

CHAPTER 11

TRANSLATION OF LATIN HYMNS
see Neale, chapter 1 above
Connelly, Joseph, ed. and trans., *Hymns of the Roman Liturgy*,
   London, Longmans, Green, 1957

TOPICAL INDEX